Making the
Most of
Retirement

The Daily Telegraph

LIFEPLANNER

Making the Most of
Retirement

Michael
Barratt

**KOGAN
PAGE**

5003935.32

First published in 1999

Kogan Page Limited
120 Pentonville Road
London N1 9JN

British Library Cataloguing in Publication Data

A CIP record for this book is available from the British Library.

ISBN 0 7494 2826 0

Typeset by JS Typesetting, Wellingborough, Northants
Printed and bound in Great Britain by Thanet Press Ltd, Margate

Renewing your home insurance?

If you are aged 50 or over you will find Saga Home Insurance well worth looking into. With an unrivalled knowledge of our customers and their requirements, our home insurance policies have been developed to meet your needs, in short, exceptional levels of cover and outstanding value for money.

High quality cover at competitive prices
Saga Home Insurance covers a wide range of properties and up to £50,000 contents as standard. Our easy one-call claims service means there are normally no forms to fill in, while our 24-hour helplines provide practical advice on domestic emergencies and legal matters. Add to this our accidental damage cover, continuous cover when you are away from home for up to 60 days, plus extra contents cover at Christmas and to coincide with family weddings, and you will see it gives you real peace of mind.

If you are over 50, call Saga today for a quotation or instant cover

SAGA
Now's the time

☎ FREE **0800 414 525**

quoting reference GP6914

Our lines are open 8.30am-7pm weekdays, 9am-1pm Saturday
Telephone calls may be monitered/recorded for staff training purposes

At Peter Harris Racing Stables You Don't Just Own A Racehorse - You Share In The Pendley Way Of Life.

Virtually unique in racing circles and unlike many anonymous clubs and syndicates, owners at Peter Harris Racing Stables can really be involved in the progress of their horse.

They form partnerships, naming their horse, as well as choosing their own unique racing colours.

Owners Welcomed At The Stables

Owners, their families and friends are welcomed and have free rein of the stables at Pendley Farm, 7 days a week, where they can see every aspect of racing from breeding to training, (a unique opportunity).

Stunning Facilities

Pendley, set in 800 acres of prime Hertfordshire countryside, has excellent facilities for you and your guests, providing the perfect backdrop for watching your horse develop from tentative steps on the lunge rein, to serious work on the gallops.

You can also be sure Peter Harris has designed the perfect location for bringing on horses of all abilities, maximising their full potential.

A Racing Enthusiast's Paradise

Pendley Farm is the racing enthusiast's paradise. And to gain entry you don't need to invest any capital - a simple monthly payment (which can never be increased) is all it takes,

and covers all costs, including your horse purchase, training, farrier, vets, jockey and race entry fees.

Each owner also gets 2 badges to the Members' enclosure on race days.

Plus you will receive your share of all winnings *and* your share of the value of your horse when sold.

Does all this sound too good to be true? Where's the catch? There isn't one.

For the complete picture contact us to receive your FREE introductory video.

FOR MORE INFORMATION
TEL : 01442 826393

Please send me your FREE video

Tel Day :

Tel Eve :

NAME

ADDRESS

Postcode   DTR6/99

PETER HARRIS RACING STABLES, PENDLEY FARM, TRING, HERTS, HP23 5RS

Contents

*dear grandma
I hope you will be
happy in your
new home...*

love

Emma xxx

Retirement Homesearch is the specialist in the resale of Retirement properties in England, Wales and Scotland, with an unrivalled selection of retirement apartments, cottages and bungalows within developments in city, town, country and coastal locations nationwide. The majority of developments benefit from a resident House Manager, emergency call response, enhanced security, a range of communal facilities and optional value added services, all with the highest standards of property management.

For your free copy of our Nationwide Retirement Homesearch listing with over 1,000 properties for sale.

Call our retirement property specialists on:

0345 697151 (local rate)

Or write to Peverel Retirement Homesearch, FREEPOST (BH1044) New Milton, BH25 5ZZ

Retirement HOMESEARCH

www.retirementhomesearch.co.uk

Enjoy your independence with McCarthy & Stone

When the time comes to move, you won't have to give up your independence with McCarthy & Stone. Choosing one of our brand new retirement flats gives you everything you need - security, peace of mind and companionship when you want it. Yet, with your own front door key, you can remain as independent as you please. Find out for yourself, call free for further details.

SOUTH WEST
FREEPHONE 0800 919132

WILTSHIRE - Warminster, Salisbury, Swindon,
AVON - Bristol,
SOMERSET - Minehead
BATH & N. EAST SOMERSET - Bath,
DEVON - Exeter, Exmouth, Newton Abbot, Paignton, St Marychurch (Torquay), Teignmouth
DORSET - Bournemouth (Southbourne), Christchurch, Swanage
GLOUCESTERSHIRE - Gloucester
HAMPSHIRE - Alton, Fareham, Gosport, Southsea
OXFORDSHIRE - Abingdon, Banbury
SOUTH GLAMORGAN - Cardiff

SOUTH EAST
FREEPHONE 0500 870454

BEDFORDSHIRE - Leighton Buzzard,
BERKSHIRE - Caversham
ESSEX - Chelmsford, Clacton on Sea, Frinton on Sea, Halstead, Hornchurch, Rayleigh, Witham, Westcliff-on-Sea
HERTFORDSHIRE - Bishops Stortford, Potters Bar
KENT - Birchington, Canterbury, Folkestone, Southborough, Westgate on Sea
GT. LONDON - Grove Park, Muswell Hill
MIDDLESEX - Feltham, Shepperton
EAST SUSSEX - Eastbourne,
WEST SUSSEX - Chichester, Rustington
SURREY - Bagshot, Caterham-on-the-Hill, Epsom, Ewell, Wallington

NORTHERN
FREEPHONE 0500 006565

CHESHIRE - Frodsham, Stockton Heath
CLEVELAND - Middlesbrough
COUNTY DURHAM - Darlington
CUMBRIA - Grange over Sands
HEREFORDSHIRE - Ross on Wye
LANCASHIRE - Lancaster, St Annes
MERSEYSIDE - Birkdale, Southport
NORTHUMBERLAND - Morpeth
SHROPSHIRE - Shrewsbury
TYNE & WEAR - Lowfell
WIRRAL - West Kirby
YORKSHIRE - Harrogate, Ilkley, Leeds

MIDLANDS
FREEPHONE 0800 521276

BIRMINGHAM - Hall Green, Rubery
CAMBRIDGESHIRE - St Neots
LINCOLNSHIRE - Lincoln
NORFOLK - Norwich
NORTHANTS - Northampton
NOTTS - Radcliffe on Trent
SUFFOLK - Ipswich
WARWICKSHIRE - Rugby

McCARTHY & STONE

THE NATURAL CHOICE
FOR A HAPPY RETIREMENT

The Royal Society of St. George

Founded 1894
Incorporated by Royal Charter
Patron: Her Majesty the Queen
President: George R.A. Andrews Esq.
FCIB FCIS FCIArb
Chairman: William R. Firth Esq.

Are You English ?

Are you proud of your Country and of her glorious history and heritage ? Then why not become a member of The Royal Society of St. George ? You could take an active part in our mission to safeguard England and Englishness, to revitalise our nation and restore decency and integrity to our daily lives. The Royal Society of St. George aims to:

- Spark a renewed interest in our English history and traditions;
- Celebrate the glorious achievements of our past English leaders, heroes, artists and innovators;
- Promote the shared cultural heritage of the Commonwealth and all English-speaking countries;
- Encourage high standards of decency, courtesy and good manners;
- Foster self-discipline, courage and a sense of adventure, especially in our young people;
- Undertake educational projects for the furtherance of traditional English values and principles;
- Under the banner of St. George, through a Charitable Trust, provide guidance and sponsorship for young people, to assist in their personal endeavours as future leaders of the community.

Contact the address below for a brochure and a membership form:
The Royal Society of St. George,
127 Sandgate Road, Folkestone, Kent CT20 2BH.
Tel: 01303 241795   Fax: 01303 850162
Website: www.royalsocietyofstgeorge.com
E-mail: info@rssg.u-net.com

Blades of Class

Hayter lawnmowers have been maintaining great British lawns for over fifty years, since pioneering the rotary mower, putting high quality lawn care within the reach of every gardener.

With a range of innovative models, from the renowned Harrier for the classic striped lawn, to the rugged hardworking Heritage tractors, all Hayters have in common incomparable engineering and superb value for money.

Phone us for a FREE colour brochure today.

HAYTER
MAKERS OF THE FINEST MOWERS

BY APPOINTMENT TO
HER MAJESTY THE QUEEN
MANUFACTURERS OF
AGRICULTURAL MACHINERY
HAYTER LIMITED

FREEPHONE BROCHURE LINE 0800 374478
HAYTER LIMITED
Spellbrook, Bishop's Stortford, Herts CM23 4BU, England Tel: 01279 723444 Fax: 01279 600338
www.hayter.co.uk

Introduction

Let's be clear from the start. This is an optimistic book. It sees the years after retirement as years of opportunity – years to take up exciting new challenges rather than years to begin some kind of gentle decline.

So, if your idea of bliss is to stop working, put your feet up and enjoy the luxury of doing absolutely nothing, I shouldn't bother to read on.

However, don't worry: I'm not going to advocate jumping out of bed at the crack of dawn every day to do your exercises followed by a mad round of desperately 'healthy' activity. And I'm certainly not insensitive to the handicaps that many of us suffer long before reaching our 60s and 70s. It's sadly far from unusual to be saddled with, say, arthritis or other physical restrictions; to have to face up to the fact that one's mind isn't sharp enough any longer to pursue some intellectual pleasures; to experience financial hardship with an inadequate pension. All these and many more problems of older people are much in mind as I propose ways of making the years ahead both fruitful and pleasurable.

You will find no complaints from me that 'things aren't what they used to be' – though I must say that the word 'retirement' means something quite different nowadays from what it did a decade or two ago. In the past, it was assumed to mean arriving at the age of 60 for women and 65 for men. Nowadays, it's not uncommon for those in established salaried jobs to retire on company pensions as early as 50. So there's some guidance for the youngsters among us, too!

I've had a lot of fun researching detail for the following pages. And a number of surprises – like the discovery that the growing influence of the over-65s in society seems not to have been appreciated yet by the commercial world. In the leisure sector, for example, most of the major new investment in developing amenities is still directed at the young (those in their 20s and 30s) in the belief that they're the ones with money to burn. This view, I suppose, is partly explained by the fact that such a big proportion of advertising and marketing 'experts' are themselves of that age group.

Yet the average age of the nation grows daily, as does the proportion of retired people (which is one reason why the National Health Service has to keep running just to stand still). Retired individuals may be a little more careful – and selective – in their spending, but they are an increasing power in the land of commercial opportunity – so why aren't their interests and needs better catered for?

Mind you, the ideas I put forward in this book are by no means dependent on money. It's perfectly possible to develop new activities and pleasures without spending anything at all. Indeed, if your only income is the state pension, this last approach is almost essential.

For some lucky people – and I'm one of them – the dividing line between work and play is blurred. My delight is in writing, performing and directing for radio and television, that sort of thing. So, if I arrived at some kind of formal retirement, I'd look forward to having time to pursue my hobbies, which are precisely the same as the 'jobs' I've done every day since I was a teenager!

So, there never comes a day in our lives when people like me suddenly 'stop work' although, of course, there's a gradual onset of old age, which puts physical and mental restrictions on what we're able to do. In that sense, we need to be sensible and map out for ourselves working targets that take into account our more limited capabilities. It can be difficult to be realistic when doing this because none of

us likes to admit declining powers, but if we attempt work-
loads that can't be fulfilled our potential employers will very
quickly bring us down to earth with a bump.

However, there's an optimistic aspect even in this respect:
in some ways, work can become _easier_ the older we get. My
friend Rolf Harris made this point to me as we discussed
his own 'comeback' in his mid-60s. His career had looked
as if it was drawing to a close and he had become depressed
by the axing of his long-running television cartoon series.
Then, out of the blue, came the opportunity for him to
present a new TV series – _Animal Hospital_. Almost overnight,
he became a star second time round – and his depression
was swept away by a fresh enthusiasm and energy.

'I found that I could record programmes in half the time
they used to take me and with considerably less effort,
simply because I had all those years of experience under
my belt', he told me. The priceless reservoir of practical
knowledge (which we all have by the time we reach that
age) more than compensated for the other factors of advancing years. Producers needed fewer 'takes' because Rolf got
it right first time and the people (even the animals!) he
worked with responded to his skilled handling.

So, in planning how to make the most of your active years
ahead, don't make the mistake of devaluing yourself.

And don't make life more difficult, or advancing years
more oppressive, by perceiving yourself as older than you
really are! In my view, one of the biggest mistakes older
people make is to take upon themselves a mantle of 'senior-
ity', which is extremely tiresome for everybody else and
which robs them of fresh and challenging outlooks. In
particular they make it clear that they should command
something called 'respect' for their age. They want to lecture
young people rather than listen to them. They shut their
minds off from new ideas. I'm not suggesting that we should
pretend to be what we're not, or that we should dress like
teenagers or attempt recreations that are beyond our physical

abilities. However, there is no question that retaining the will both to carry on learning and to share the fun of discovery with younger people will make retirement a whole lot more fulfilling and pleasurable.

Most of you reading this book, I suppose, will be doing so from a rather more conventional standpoint than mine. After 40 or so years of Monday-to-Friday work for an employer, retirement day arrives with a handshake from the boss, a farewell party in the local hostelry, a present marking the years of faithful service... and then you're on your own, plunged into a new life that holds goodness-knows-what prospects. Now's the time when decisions have to be made about your future, rather in the same way as the management of a company prepare a business plan.

The basic difference is that the commodity you're now dealing with is not money but *time*. How are you going to spend it? What's the mix of work and leisure you'd like to achieve? Where do you want to live? How are you going to extend the time available by maintaining good health? Do you want to make provision for charity work or community service? Are you satisfied with the income from your pension and other sources or do you want to consider ways of adding to your resources?

No two people have the same answers to these questions (all of which are considered in the following pages) but there are some general principles that can help in coming to the kind of decisions you need to take. Like choosing where to live, for instance.

In different sections of this book we look at factors like your home as a financial asset or the possible pleasures (and dangers) of moving to the sun overseas. For many people, closeness to children and grandchildren is an obviously important concern here – well, for happy families, anyway! However, another consideration, and one that can easily be overlooked, is the importance of your friends. They have become such a routine part of your everyday life that they're easily forgotten when making plans to move to a smaller house, say, or a more rural location.

But you _must_ think of them – for purely selfish reasons! Finding yourself at retirement age in a new community where you have to begin all over again to make friends – and may never succeed in doing so – can be a heartbreaking experience, nullifying any other advantages from the move.

I well remember, years ago when I was reporting for _Panorama_, visiting a suburb of Liverpool where families had been rehoused – out of old, insanitary back-to-back terrace houses in cobbled streets into smart new apartments in other estates around the city. Every morning, after taking their children to school, mothers would walk or take a bus back to the old derelict houses, sit on the doorsteps, and gossip as they had always done. Friendships were stronger than bricks and mortar. I have come across examples like that again and again over the intervening years and, in particular, I have witnessed the misery of older people who have swapped their old neighbourhoods for sunnier climes abroad where days without old friends have become interminable.

More on moving matters later, when we consider the possibilities of living abroad. First, let's look at what we can afford in the years ahead; at how to make the most of what we've already accumulated in our retirement piggy banks; and at what opportunities there may be for adding to our income.

My simple guiding principle in presenting these issues for your consideration is that you know rather more about yourself and your entirely individual ambitions than I do! So my aim has been to point you in the direction of information, not to try to persuade you how to use it.

1 Money

Fact Finding

The financial scene changes daily. Chancellors legislate. Stock markets oscillate. Institutions modulate. It's all very complicated and unless money has been our business, we're none of us really capable of acquiring and understanding all the elements that will allow us to make wise choices about our personal finances.

We need help to make sensible decisions. But where is that help to be found? The most likely sources are your bank, your accountant, an independent financial adviser (IFA) or possibly your solicitor (though he or she would call upon the services of one of the others).

If you choose an IFA, whom you could find in the Yellow Pages if you don't already know one, be absolutely sure that they're properly qualified to give you sound and truly independent advice. If necessary, call the Personal Investment Authority or the Insurance Brokers Registration Council – the regulators – to establish their probity.

If you see your accountant, with whom you've had a reasonably long association, you will be confident of getting the sort of advice that understands your personal needs (and idiosyncrasies) but you will probably be charged for the time taken to give you the advice. If, on the other hand, you visit an accountant for the first time, you may not be charged at all on the basis that you're a good prospect as a new client!

If you seek the advice of the bank with which you have an account, ask to see a senior consultant. That way, you will be given completely free advice – but it will be tied to the bank in the sense that it will promote the bank's own services. However, all the main high-street banks have specialist services, which are usually called 'private banking', where you can receive truly independent help in a free consultation. If, as a result of that meeting, you decide to ask them to manage your money for you, then there will naturally be a fee.

A senior manager of Lloyds Bank (who had just been given early retirement and was therefore even closer to the challenge of maximising assets at this stage in life!) told me:

'In looking at each individual's needs, the first thing we have to consider is their attitude to risk. If they are looking for ways to boost income with the best possible safety and security, we suggest they consider interest-earning accounts at the bank, National Savings, that sort of thing. But perhaps they're prepared to seek higher returns, in which case we'll steer them in other directions while making sure that they understand the modest risks involved.

'But whatever their preferences, we can only give the best advice if people are entirely open with us. Painful mistakes can be made if decisions are taken on the basis of incomplete or misleading information.'

It may be, of course, that the only help you need is in handling your tax affairs. In that case, don't forget that the Inland Revenue has a duty to serve you – without charge, it goes without saying, except in the sense that we're all paying for their services! The local phone directory lists all the numbers and addresses of their service offices, information centres and tax districts. You can either visit or phone them and they are duty-bound to give you the best advice on how to avoid income tax and capital gains tax. (To evade, of course, is illegal.)

It's a good idea to do some reading before you go to meet people, so you'll be better armed to understand and answer the sort of questions they'll put to you. The library and your local booksellers have shelves groaning with publications. And charitable organisations with no political or commercial bias produce all manner of guides either free or at a very modest price. One I'd strongly recommend, published by Help the Aged and sponsored by NatWest Bank, is _Managing a Lump Sum_. Its title is the only phrase in the booklet that gives a wrong impression. It's not only for those who have a pile of money to invest as it covers just about every permutation of income and expenditure that the pensioner (who may not be exactly 'aged' these days) may experience.

If you fill in the straightforward lists of incomings and outgoings, assets and debts, which are both simple and comprehensive in this booklet, you'll get a very clear picture of your real worth. You will then be able to provide one of those financial advisers mentioned above with the vital information upon which sound decisions can be made.

We all have different approaches to money matters. Some of us enjoy spending to the hilt – you can't take it with you, spend it while you can enjoy it, that kind of attitude. Others are much more cautious and want to be sure they have as much as may be needed to cover all eventualities if they live to be a hundred. Leaving as much as possible for children and grandchildren may be your quite different priority. So, it's clearly impossible to provide detailed advice here without knowing your personal needs. The important thing is to know where to find the help to 'do it your way' and that's what I've tried to signpost above. Now let's look at some ideas that may be attractive options whatever your principal motivation.

Profitable Fun

Consider first an idea that encompasses most of the aims I'm trying to achieve in this little book. It provides an interest, so that each morning, on waking, the day ahead offers at least one prospect of pleasure. It stimulates the mind. It encourages forward-looking involvement in topical issues. It can provide rewards in many ways including financial. It offers the opportunity to enlarge your circle of friends. It can take up as much or as little of your available time as you choose. And it's affordable for practically everybody. It's the Investment Club.

The idea of 'dabbling' (as cynics would put it) in stocks and shares may not appeal to you for many reasons: you may never have ventured into what seems a risky world; you may think it involves gambling money, which you can't afford to lose; you may be ignorant of how the stock market works; you may believe that becoming involved in financial investment with friends is a recipe for broken relationships – in the same way as you'd probably hesitate to sell your old car to a friend.

But investment clubs minimize risk. Membership may cost as little, or as much, as you can comfortably afford. They don't require any specialized knowledge of the market on your part (although, as we shall see, they benefit from your own experience of the job you did before you retired). And they actually strengthen and stimulate friendships, as members of literally thousands of clubs in Britain today will testify.

The idea is to get together with a few friends and acquaintances and agree to pool a small amount of money each month. As little as £10 could suffice; between £25 and £50 is typical. You give the club a name and register it with ProShare, the organization that represents the interests of private investors.

ProShare will provide you with a manual that answers hundreds of questions about how to set up, and run, an investment club. You'll meet once a month in a member's home or in some other venue that won't require any significant cost – the back room of a pub, perhaps, or the village hall. Together you'll appoint a stockbroker, who buys or sells shares for you all. The fun – and, hopefully, the profit – comes from the discussion of what to invest in.

It's very important, of course, that however friendly and convivial your meetings may be, they should be organised in an efficient and orderly fashion, so you'll need to choose a chairman, a secretary and a treasurer – all honorary, of course.

ProShare's development director, Terry Bond, says: 'One of the main objectives is, of course, to make money. But, at the same time, the meetings must be fun, social occasions where nobody's standard of living is going to be affected if a few wrong decisions are made.'

Some clubs try to avoid pressurizing members into contributions they can't afford by varying the amount paid into the kitty – £10, say, from one member and £25 from another. But this could lead to grumbling from the more affluent because investment decisions are made on a strictly democratic basis of one member, one vote, whatever one's financial contribution. Certainly ProShare's advice is for everyone to pay in the same amount.

Once the club has been established on the right lines, each meeting should be a lot of fun. Debate will be lively, ranging from those who want to 'splash out' on speculative penny shares, in the hope of making a small killing, to those cautious types who want to be as sure as possible of a stable return by investing only in blue-chip companies.

One of the most important, and satisfying, aspects of the club idea, in my view, is the fact that members will come from a whole range of backgrounds, which will enable them to contribute specialized knowledge to the debates while at the same time learning a lot from their colleagues. Terry Bond advocates making best use of this knowledge by allocating particular sectors of the stock market to individual members of groups:

'For example, a chemist will know about pharmaceuticals and a computer programmer will understand information technology. Even someone who hasn't been out to work for years but has devoted time to home and family will have a good knowledge of food retailing and fashion. Everyone has a different circle of knowledge, which means that investment decisions can be based on shared information and opinions based on personal experience.'

One good tip to add to the pleasure and interest in a club is taken from an article in *The Times*: 'You won't be able to pick a new share at every meeting, but add a frisson of excitement by asking everyone to pick a portfolio of five shares and track their performance for a month. The winner gets a free bottle of wine. Winning shares then move to the top of the list for investment.'

Investment clubs are not just for older people, of course – they're an excellent way of introducing youngsters to the mysteries of the stock market. But it seems to me that they are ideally suited to retired people looking for new interests in their daily lives.

Of course, that interest is certainly not confined to a once-a-month attendance at a club meeting. Watching the performance of shares, following the fortunes of companies, large and small, keeping up with the business news... all these are everyday occupations that can add a lot of fun to your life. If it all adds a bob or two to your income as well, then it's a significant bonus!

Do-it-yourself Investment

It may be that the Investment Club idea is not right for you – because you're a loner who gets more of a kick out of investing without help from your friends, perhaps, or because you're not mobile enough to get out and about.

If so, could the stock market still provide an opportunity to add fresh interest to your days of retirement and create a little extra income at the same time? If you're careful and can reasonably expect to live for another five years or more, the answer's yes.

I make that lifespan qualification because prudence dictates that you should only begin to invest in the market if you're spending money that you can do without for at least five years. In other words, you shouldn't be tempted into speculating with money you need for everyday living expenses.

In the long term, the stock market will give you a better return on your money than any other form of investment or saving. It's been calculated, for instance, that if you had placed £100 in a bank savings account 70 years ago, it would be worth £7,000 in today's money. Placed in gilt-edged securities it would have grown to £9,000. Invested in stocks and shares through a 'tracker fund' (which keeps close tabs on the daily performance of major shares) it would now stand at £710,000.

Put another way, statistics show that if you examine any ten-year period during your lifetime, the market has far outperformed any other form of investment. But the key phrase in that sentence is 'ten-year period' because, of course, the market fluctuates – sometimes dramatically – and so short-term investment could result in a painful loss. That's why the relentless advertising by financial institutions always carries warnings like: 'The value of an investment in a unit trust and the income from it can go down as well as up. It may be affected by exchange rate variations, and you may not get back the amount invested.'

But, having paid heed to all the warnings, there's still a lot to be said for developing your stock market knowledge as an enjoyable hobby, and a profitable one at that, especially if you're starting from a base of fairly early retirement – say, 60 years of age – which means that reasonably long-term planning is practical.

Obviously you'll want to do your homework first. (Sticking a pin in a list of names, as you might when having a little flutter on a horse race, is a recipe for disaster.) And there are many sources of information worth seeking, especially if you go for quality – in other words, respected high-street names and institutions.

It's likely that your local authority runs further education courses in financial management. The big banks all stage or sponsor talks and seminars on investment. ProShare's Terry Bond (quoted earlier) regularly gives talks around the country, providing really basic advice for the absolute beginner. Companies like Marks & Spencer will gladly supply details of their share-tracker funds.

Two books to give you a solid start to your new hobby are: the Investors Chronicle *Personal Finance Planner* by Debbie Harrison (Pitman) and *The Investor's Handbook – ProShare's No-nonsense Guide to Sensible Investing* (Batsford). And, of course, there's also lots to learn from another title in the *Daily Telegraph*'s Lifeplanner series: *Guide to Lump Sum Investment* by Liz Walkington (Kogan Page, 1999).

Asset Rich?

Wealth can be measured in a hundred different ways. Personal ways. Some people aspire to 'the good life' in retirement, spending freely the money saved during the earning years as a sort of much-deserved reward for all that hard work. Others still worry about security and are concerned to continue saving as much as possible 'for a rainy day'. Some plan to maximize their assets for passing on to their children and grandchildren – or even to the cat-and-dog home! Yet others take pleasure simply in increasing their wealth as an end in itself, rather like a game of Monopoly.

There's no financial advice that suits everybody and certainly no right or wrong way to handle personal resources. Consider, for example, the asset that many people have on reaching retirement – the home they own. By any standards, it is worth a substantial amount of money (say, £100,000 for a modest semi). The mortgage will have been paid off over perhaps 25 years of employment and it's certainly a great comfort to know that it's your unassailable castle for the rest of your life.

But what if your cash income is no more than a basic pension, giving you only the bare necessities of life with nothing left over each week to enjoy the pleasures of the retirement years like holidays, cinema and theatre outings and visiting family and relations? What would you say, then, to the idea of turning some of the bricks and mortar into spending money, while still living in your home for the rest of your life?

You can unlock some of the money tied up in your home through a variety of schemes, usually called HIPs (Home Income Plans). They're not as easy to come by as they once were (possibly because a number of building societies and other institutions found them to be poor profit earners) but they're still on offer if you shop around.

Basically, a HIP means that homeowners take out a fresh mortgage that is then used to pay for an annuity – providing a regular guaranteed income that will never reduce (apart from income-tax rates) for the rest of their lives. Part of the income has to be used to pay the interest on the loan, but the remainder is yours for the 'extras' you wouldn't other-wise be able to afford.

It's an attractive proposition if you're strapped for cash – but do make sure you know all the downside facts before rushing into any arrangement. For a start, you'd probably have difficulty finding a scheme before you're seventy. (The regular income payments increase the older you are.) Obviously, too, the HIP will require your having household insurance cover and you might find that the cover you're currently paying for is out of date and will therefore cost more. On the plus side, your home may well be worth much more than you think if you've had no call to have it valued in recent years and that will, of course, enable you to establish a higher annuity than you had imagined.

But this is by no means the only way of using your home to increase the amount of cash available for your daily life. Most simply, you may consider selling and moving to a smaller or cheaper home that you can buy outright, thus leaving a tidy cash sum for spending or investing. (There could be a further bonus from such a move – the challenge of turning the new property into your retirement dream home with some DIY activity that could keep you stimulated and pleasantly busy for months!)

You can acquire much more useful advice on 'cashing in' on your home through publications produced by the charities Age Concern and Help the Aged (addresses at the end of this book).

Value Added?

Whatever your job before retirement, you have been of real value to those who have paid for your services. Either you've had a regular wage/salary or you have been paid fees for your services. (Even unemployed people are able to supplement their welfare payments.)

The day you retire, that value does not suddenly cease, even if the 'weekly wage' does. You still have something to offer somebody somewhere. Indeed, it is arguable that, in some respects, you now have added value: you have a lifetime's working experience; you have a kind of independence that may make your advice worth more than it was when you needed to toe the company line; you no longer represent a costly 'overhead' to an employer who, up to now, has needed to provide you with an office, perhaps a car, a pension contribution and all the rest.

In particular – and paradoxically, it may seem – the ever-increasing accent on youth in employment, with early retirement being common practice, may prove a blessing in disguise. It's not at all uncommon nowadays to hear business people saying something like: 'We get good service from our suppliers, with some very bright young people using state-of-the-art technology to service our needs – but we do miss the experience and wisdom of the older ones whose advice we valued so much.'

That means they're missing you! And, therefore, there is a growing market for your experience.

There are many ways in which you can exploit this opportunity. If you're a natural entrepreneur with a flair for selling yourself, why not set up a consultancy offering your expertise to companies who could profit from your advice? All you need is a desk at home, a telephone and some headed notepaper – though it will make you more efficient if you are able to afford other aids like a fax machine and a computer with e-mail.

In your own industry or profession, you'll probably have easy access to reference books providing details of companies worth approaching to offer your services. (There's always the public library if you haven't.)

If you decide to pursue this idea, the most important initial activity is thinking. In other words, don't rush into spraying letters around your chosen business sector. Begin by thinking through what it is you genuinely have to offer that can make you attractive to a potential client – the marketing jargon is USP (Unique Selling Proposition). Then consider the kind of companies that, in your past experience, really have a need for your special talents. Only then, when you're quite clear in your mind what your specific targets should be, do you set about marketing your services.

The way you do that – by writing letters or making phone calls or networking by developing social contacts – will depend to some degree on your own personality. Are you a natural salesman who enjoys the art of persuasion on a personal basis, for instance, or are your communication skills more effective through writing?

However you set about it, you're able in retirement to devote just as much or as little time to developing a consultancy as you please, without any of the pressures of making a living in the 'working years'. You can simply decide, say, to put aside a couple of hours a day in the first instance while you seek clients – or to spend most of your time in a determined effort to get your enterprise off the ground. And when you succeed in finding an interested client, you still have the enviable freedom of being able to negotiate just how much time you want to spend on carrying out the work. Thus, you can propose a monthly fee, which you estimate will cover your spending the equivalent of a day a week on the account, or agree an hourly rate of payment. Either way will not tie you down so much that the freedom of retirement and the opportunity to pursue other activities (like some advocated later in this book) are eroded.

But experience is not the only asset you enjoy in retirement: free time, to use just as you please, means that you have the opportunity to pursue other, new activities, which may bring added sources of income as well as pleasure. Adult education could be the door to acquiring new skills that, in turn, mean earning money. A catering course could lead to the establishment of a nice little business serving social events in your locality. A gardening course could spawn another obvious service: there's always a call for it in most communities and it doesn't have to mean sweated labour. Office skills are always in demand and could equip you as a valuable 'temp', able to choose the hours you're available for work.

The other approach to finding retirement work may be called the reactive one – responding to the opportunities that will undoubtedly be presented to you. (Appeals to you to help various charitable activities without financial reward are considered separately in a later section. Here we're looking at money-earning options.)

You now have more time than before to peruse part-time job appointments advertised in your newspapers and magazines. There are more than there used to be, especially as employers have become much more attuned to the idea of people working for them from home.

And there are increasing opportunities to apply to so-called quangos. In days gone by, these bodies were famous (or infamous) for providing easy-money rewards for political favours, for perpetuating the 'old boy network'. But nowadays great efforts are being made to recruit ordinary people with special interests or experience (and with spare time) to serve on quasi-government committees in all fields of life – social services, the law, education and so on. Indeed, it is rare to pick up, say, a Sunday newspaper nowadays without finding at least one such advertisement.

Seeking new, paid work in retirement clearly has other financial implications, not least the consequential income tax. That's not something to be discussed here in any detail because there are as many different circumstances to be considered as there are readers of this book. The tax regime changes each year, anyhow. And you will have your own attitude to taxation. Like me, you may wish you paid more tax because it can only mean that you're earning more money, but there are those of you who have a passion for avoiding tax and who may feel in consequence that extra work in retirement is not worth the candle.

In any case, it's worth considering the basic options and how you can be helped to make a wise and informed choice.

2 Activity

There are countless ways of enjoying – and prolonging – retirement according to personal choice and circumstances. But I am certain that there is one absolute necessity if you want to be happy and live longer: to be active physically or mentally or, ideally, both. We all know people who have literally 'died of boredom' after finishing work and having nothing to put in its place. Even if you have made reasonable provision for your financial security, that will be of little comfort if you have no good reason to look forward to each day as a fresh challenge with fresh activities in prospect.

So now let's examine the possibilities. In the pages that follow I make no attempt to be selective or to prefer any one activity to another. One man's meat is another man's poison in this, as in so much else to do with choosing our post-retirement lifestyle. So here's a random selection of suggested activities – starting almost at the end of the alphabetical list, a W!

Stroll On

The simplest activity of all, surely, and arguably the most rewarding, is walking. It needn't cost you a penny. It's something everybody can enjoy (including, as we shall see, the disabled). It can be pursued anywhere at any time, on your own or in company. And it will almost certainly extend your lifespan.

At the simplest level, a two-mile walk taking just over half an hour before breakfast each morning will set you up for the day. In town or country there's always something new to observe, so it's far from boring, even if you take the same route each day. (It also gets the metabolism up and running so that you can benefit to the full from that breakfast, which is so much more enjoyable when you get back to the kitchen with roses in your cheeks!)

If you're particularly keen to develop your fitness level then you may adopt walking as a rather more serious business and develop a faster pace over longer periods. In his book, _Fit for Life_ (Little, Brown and Company, London), Ranulph Fiennes commends a step-by-step regimen that will have you eventually walking three miles in 36 minutes – that's five miles an hour – three times a week to maintain what he regards as a 'reasonable' level of fitness. He tells you to 'swing your arms forward with aggression... breathe as normally and regularly as possible... keep your back straight'.

Yes, well, you may find all that a little excessive if you seek rather gentler enjoyment! In that case, I'd recommend your talking to the Ramblers' Association who publish a series of brochures and leaflets. These publications underline just how simple it is to explore the countryside along miles and miles of public footpaths or, if you're a townie, how and where to discover canal towpaths, riverside walks, walking trails, commons and heaths.

If you haven't arranged a full schedule of other interests to pursue each day (which is quite possible by the time you have reached the end of this book) you may find that walking begins to develop as a hobby and that you'd like to pursue it more energetically. Thus:

If you are uncertain about map-reading or following a guidebook's directions, or just unsure about walking in the countryside generally, perhaps the best way for you to start is by joining experienced ramblers on an organized group

For Those Who've Ever Dreamt
The Celebrated Trainer Peter

A lot of horseracing's followers spend their life dreaming of owning a racehorse.

Mention to them a name like Ascot, Epsom, Newmarket or York, and it will conjure up highly personal visions of racing which, likely as not, will include a glamourous social occasion, the popping of champagne corks and lathered equine athletes!

Their vision will also show that to participate fully in this racing world, requires you to be royalty, or rich, (preferably both). Until now, that is.

Because, set in 800 acres of prime Hertfordshire countryside near Tring, is Peter Harris Racing Stables, where there's a mini revolution happening in racehorse ownership.

What Peter has managed to do is place racehorse ownership within the reach of racing's real enthusiasts.

Unlike anonymous racing clubs, where there could be up to a thousand members, or syndicates where a large capital deposit is required, Peter has created a partnership system where owners need no deposit and pay by simple fixed monthly payments.

What's more the payment can never be increased, and includes the horse purchase, vet's bills, farrier's bills, jockey fees and race entry fees.

In fact, there are absolutely no other hidden extras, which means you know exactly how much you will pay, (and by how many payments), before signing up.

Each partnership gets to name their horse and choose their own unique racing colours.

And each owner is also entitled to 2 badges to the Member's enclosure on race days plus their share of all winnings and their share of the value of their horse when sold.

But it's not only the financial package that makes Peter Harris Racing Stables unique, it's the fact that all

About Owning Their Own Racehorse, Harris Makes It An Affordable

owners, their friends and families have free rein of the stables, 7 days a week.

At Pendley Farm, where the stables are based, you can use the extensive

facilities to enjoy every aspect of owning a racehorse, from its first tentative steps on the lunge rein to serious work on the gallops.

You'll also meet people from all walks of life. People who share the same passion as yourself. And by visiting as often as you like, you can watch your horse develop and feel completely involved in its training.

You'll experience the infectious enthusiasm the stable lads and lasses

have for their charges too, and the care and thought that Peter has put into designing the perfect location for bringing on horses of all abilities, maximising each one's full potential.

Needless to say, as a trainer, Peter is well known and celebrated within racing circles.

Last season he had 37 winners, 37 seconds, and 35 thirds - earning a total of £360,000 for his owners. A record that improves year on year.

It's difficult though, in such a short article to get across the true spirit and character of the stables.

A visit to Peter Harris Racing Stables therefore is highly recommended.

So if we've whetted your appetite, call 01442 826393 for more details.

walk. The Ramblers' Association has over 400 groups around Britain, and each arranges its own year-round programme of walks. Naturally the walks vary in terms of length and overall difficulty (although most are nothing more than simple and enjoyable countryside rambles!).

In addition to Ramblers' Association groups, there are many other independent walking clubs that organize regular walks, mostly for their members, and in popular outdoor areas there are often officially organized outings – such as in the National Parks of England and Wales, which have regular programmes of guided, daily walks for the public.

(The Ramblers' Association, information literature, 1998)

More ambitiously still, you could graduate to following some of the National Trails created by the Countryside Commission. If you wanted to walk some of these, you'd have to take a fairly long break from home: the Pennine Way is more than 250 miles long and the South West Coast Path about 600 miles! You could even go rambling abroad through one of the holiday operators like Countryside and Ramblers Holidays.

I wrote earlier that even disabled people can enjoy walking, and I was thinking particularly of another Ramblers' Association initiative called 'Let's Get Going', which issues guidelines for walking with visually impaired people; those with learning difficulties; wheelchair users and others with limited mobility; epileptics; the deaf and hard of hearing. If you come into any of those categories, help is at hand for you to explore the countryside. If you're fit and agile, you might think it a fulfilling occupation to lend a hand.

Exclusively for people aged 50 and over, Saga walking holidays make sure you don't take on more than you want to – or than your body can sensibly cope with. So they classify each holiday in one of three grades – up to 6 miles on easy, fairly level ground; up to 8 miles with undulating paths and comfortable gradients; up to 11 miles including moderate hills.

A host or local leader, who carries a mobile telephone and is accompanied by a back-marker, leads all the walks. You may think that's taking mollycoddling a bit too far, especially for responsible adults like you – but even the 'safe' pleasures of walking require sensible precautions.

If you do indulge in rather more demanding rambling activities than taking the dog for a brisk walk round the neighbourhood, it's also more pleasurable to take some care with choosing clothing and footwear that will provide both protection and comfort. As I never wear a hat, I was struck by this advice in the Ramblers' Association fact sheet:

'Up to 40 per cent of body heat is lost through the head, so it is essential to protect your head and ears. A woolly hat is a must in winter, certainly if you are venturing into the hills, and it can be worn under an anorak hood. But the head is also vulnerable to the sun's rays in the warmer months, so it is important to carry a sunhat or light headscarf (and apply sun cream).'

In the Garden

I met a friend in the pub who had recently retired from a busy, well-paid and even glamorous life as an airline pilot. He was bemoaning the weather, which was preventing his having his usual daily round of golf.

'What do you do all day now that you're retired and can't get out on the golf course?' I asked him.

He sighed and looked deeply depressed. 'Oh, watch the television – racing fills in the afternoons – and generally sit around. Do a bit of gardening if I have to. But I hate gardening!'

It was my turn to be depressed. What a way to face possibly 20 or more years. It also struck me that his idea of gardening is probably shared by many: cutting the lawn, weeding, clearing up the leaves in autumn and, worst of all, digging.

But it doesn't have to be like that. Believe it or not, gardening can be fun and, properly planned, can be a welcome addition to retirement activities even if you start off with no basic horticultural knowledge.

I was lucky enough to spend five years as chairman of *Gardeners' Question Time* on BBC Radio and I learnt from those wonderfully witty green-fingered gentlemen Bill Sowerbutts, Fred Loads and Alan Gemmell. In particular, I learnt how gardening can embrace a variety of interests and skills that don't call for the backbreaking boredom my friend hates so much.

Indeed, it could be argued that the best day for gardening is when you can't get out of the house because you're ill or the weather's too bad. That's the day to swap your spade for pencil and paper. I've even heard it argued that they're the most valuable tools you possess, because a garden that's a joy to behold, and to cultivate, is the product of thoughtful design in the first place.

Many people, of course, retire to apartments or flats because there are no longer family demands on extra bedrooms or because they want to cut the daily housework down to a minimum. That may mean there's no garden to cultivate – but don't forget that local authorities have a statutory obligation to provide land for allotments, so you can still have a patch of your own.

If you have moved into a new home that has its own garden area, then you may be starting from scratch with no more than a 'plot', which the builders have left for you to design as you please. Or you may move into an older house where the garden has been so neglected that you really need to start all over again.

Anyway, whatever the circumstances, the fun begins with that pencil and paper as you work out the garden of your retirement dreams – anything from a mostly paved area with a few hardy annuals adding colour, so that you'll have the minimum of physical effort in the years ahead, to something much more challenging and absorbing, which will actually encourage you to spend an hour or two most days, growing flowers or vegetables or both.

There's a fascinating list of factors to learn about and then take into consideration at this planning stage: local conditions like the type of soil, temperature, rainfall, degree of shelter from winds and frosts, whether your plot is sloping or flat and so on. There may be local by-laws to consider – rules in open-plan estates, for instance, about the height or the nature of hedges and fences that can (or can't) be placed around your plot. And if you have next-door neighbours, you'll want to avoid some construction that's going to turn your coming years into a long nightmare of bad relations!

As in so many other activities, the great joy now is that gardening can take up precisely as much or as little of your time as you please. As one of your chosen major hobbies, it can be wonderfully rewarding. On the other hand, some sensible design work could produce an area with some easy chairs for summer afternoon relaxation, with no need to lift a fork in anger throughout the year.

If you want to make a serious effort to learn more about gardening, the opportunities are endless. There are almost as many gardening books around in shops and libraries as there are cookery titles (and that's saying something). It's impossible to choose between most of them, but I can't resist recommending the 'Be Your Own Gardening Expert' series, written by Dr. D.G. Hessayon and published by pbi Publications, which you can buy in garden centres as well as bookshops. The author has the ability to transmit detailed and comprehensive information in fewer words than you'd believe possible – a wonderful skill that I have long envied! There are day- and night-school courses in most areas. Under the auspices of the National Trust and similar bodies there are famous gardens to visit and to wonder at. You can become a Fellow of the Royal Horticultural Society, which sounds marvellously impressive but actually means no more than you've joined and paid the subscription. Seriously, though, it does open doors to increasing your knowledge substantially through its publications, lectures, visits to the great gardens at Wisley in Surrey, priority attendance at the world-famous Chelsea Flower Show and much more besides.

In addition, there are many specialist societies covering almost everything from alpine gardens to cacti and succulents, from the National Vegetable Society to nerines and orchids.

You can even pursue your hobby into the competitive world of the local flower and vegetable show as you strive for the perfect pelargonium or the longest leek. And you can keep trying as long as you live, which I suppose makes gardening an added attraction for you senior citizens.

Sharing Skills

Some time ago, when I was producing a video for VSO (Voluntary Service Overseas) in St Lucia in the Caribbean, I came across an English retired couple who were having the time of their lives. Back home, he had been a carpenter and she a teacher. Here they were now, doing much the same jobs (though in a dramatically different environment) as volunteers.

I was surprised to meet them because all my experience of VSO until then had been with young people. (Indeed, my wife had been a volunteer in her early 20s in Fiji and she still counts it as one of the most fulfilling periods of her life.) I assumed that VSO recruited only adventurous youngsters who wanted to combine 'charitable' work for poorer countries overseas with a desire to 'see the world' before settling down to normal adult life back home.

I couldn't have been more wrong – and, in particular, I had a lot to learn about the important role that retired people could play in the modern VSO movement. It offers, in my view, a wonderful opportunity for retired people (under 70) to bring a whole new dimension to their lives with a fresh challenge, memorable experiences, travel, a chance to make full use of the skills acquired during their working lives, the satisfaction of helping needy communities throughout the world – and possibly adding to their bank balances at the same time. That's quite a catalogue of bonuses!

A very useful explanatory leaflet puts it this way:

> We see VSO volunteers as people who share our values. They all seek adventure, enjoy challenge and are motivated by the prospect of living and working in a community with a very different outlook. Qualified in their particular fields of work, they want to share their skills by doing a real job from day one. In return, they receive a modest financial package and accommodation... plus the experience of a lifetime.
>
> However, despite these common features, there is no stereo-typical volunteer. VSO volunteers are a diverse group of people coming from all walks of life. They come from a range of ethnic and national backgrounds (including those recruited from Canada, the Netherlands and Portugal) and cover a wide range of occupations and professions.
>
> The VSO concept is to provide help where it's most needed – in local communities, sharing knowledge and different ways of working, respecting other cultures and traditions and providing training in specific skills – all in a spirit of mutual growth. Through these ideals we aim to make a visible improvement to people's lives overseas – whether in education, health, their income and employment opportunities, or their ability to contribute to society.

> (VSO, information literature, 1998)

The range of employment backgrounds covers all manner of professions from accountancy and agriculture to brick-laying, journalism, midwifery, specialist teaching, music, irrigation engineering and a hundred more besides. Typically, the organization requires a formal qualification (if one exists) and at least two years' experience. Obviously, it's also important when filling vacancies in intemperate climates and conditions that candidates are in good health.

And as I said, a VSO posting can actually enhance your financial position. If you're one of the five thousand or so people who apply each year and are selected for interview (they call it 'assessment') your travel and out-of-pocket expenses will be paid. If you're successful, your return flight and visa or permit will be paid in full. Before you set off on the normal two-year assignment, you'll be given a grant of around £500. (These figures are correct as this book goes to print but you will, of course, want to check them out for yourself if you proceed with an application.) Another grant of around £300 will be given half way through your placement – and a further £1,500 when you complete the job and return home.

All the time you're overseas, you will receive a modest living allowance (often the same rate as local people doing a similar job). And, of course, all this is in addition to the regular pension you receive anyway. You'll also be covered by VSO's medical expenses. If you own your own house in the UK, you can consider letting it for the two-year period to add further to your income while you're away. So, you're not exactly being asked to make a financial sacrifice!

The couple I met in St. Lucia had the best of all worlds because they had different skills, both of which were needed in the school where they were working – and that meant that they were both volunteers who could continue to live together. But it's not necessary for both of you to be recruited. VSO recognizes the benefits of partners (or dependants) staying together. So, the partner who isn't going to work will be welcome to share the accommodation overseas but will naturally be expected to pay his or her own travel costs and other expenses, except health insurance. But there's an exception to even that rule in locations where there are more requests for helpers than there are volunteers available.

Then, VSO may make exceptions and pay for a non-working partner's travel and expenses.

Disabled people reading all this may feel that the rigours of overseas postings and the need for good health will disqualify them from service. Not a bit of it. VSO actually has a policy of welcoming applications from people with disabilities, and application forms are available in large print and also on audiotape.

One last thought about VSO: you don't have to be an intrepid explorer sailing off into unknown perils overseas to be a Volunteer. Apart from the fact that some postings are most desirable (I'd have happily stayed on in St Lucia) there are many opportunities for retired people to contribute to the organization here at home without financial reward.

There are something like 80 groups of helpers throughout the UK, from the Scottish Highlands to Cornwall, which help to promote the work of VSO while learning about development projects all over the world. There are social events like international food evenings or world music nights to add to the fun of joining a group.

So there you are, another opportunity to share your skills with those who will really value them – and another opportunity to add a whole new meaning to your precious retirement years at the same time.

A Good Bet

Once a year, I have a bet on the Grand National. I buy more papers, read all the gossip and study the tipsters' forecasts. The family gets involved, too, with their favours usually based on the horses' names or the jockeys' colours. We watch the great race on television with mounting excitement – and, it has been known, with elation if we have a win or a place.

And, like most people, that's that until next year. But, now that you have the prospect of so much more time to indulge your whims, have you thought of racing as a sport to add interest and fresh motivation to your retirement? It's well worth considering.

Perhaps the image of horseracing is confusing: The 'sport of kings' may be thought of as a pastime only for the rich and aristocratic, with their Bentleys and big bets, or as the rather seedy preoccupation of layabouts spending their days in betting shops.

In fact, racing is becoming more and more an attractive sport for people of average means – and for the retired, who especially enjoy midweek meetings at courses all over the country.

Unlike many other sporting activities, it's not one you can easily learn about from books. They do exist, but racing people are universally adamant that the only real way to learn and develop a passion for it is by visiting courses and stables, by rubbing shoulders with others (who are usually eager to talk and share their own knowledge), by watching the horses as they go round the pre-parade ring (so that you begin to develop an eye for fitness) and by reading the papers and watching television. One lifetime racegoer said to me: 'Channel 4 has done wonders for the sport with its intelligent and comprehensive coverage including its Saturday morning racing chat show. A new follower can learn so much from it.'

Most stables have open days when you can literally learn from the horse's mouth and absorb the unique atmosphere of this world and its key people – trainers, head lads, jockeys and all the rest. There's usually a token fee asked for, which goes to charity. The best-known open days are at the famous Lambourn stables in Berkshire and the Middleham stables in Yorkshire, which occur every Good Friday. However, these venues attract huge crowds and you'd maybe be better to choose a smaller stable at a less popular time. Stables tend to be located in or near small towns and villages, and a visit to the local pub could be a pleasant way to ingratiate yourself with the local racing folk and wheedle an invitation out of them.

If your interest grows (as it almost certainly will if you are able to devote the time to it) there are other places to visit. One suggestion would be the National Stud at Newmarket, where the fascinating story of breeding is acted out by horses, each of which may be worth as much as a million pounds. Just down the road, incidentally, is the Animal Health Trust, which carries out much important research work on horses' injuries and illnesses. The Trust can offer many ways in which people with time to spare (ie to use) can help their work.

But while racing often involves big money, an interest in it can be one of the cheapest of recreations. At many courses you can enter for as little as £3 if you're a pensioner. And, of course, there's no need to place a bet in order to enjoy your afternoon.

Nor is there any charge for a helpful little 'guide to an enjoyable day at the races' entitled _Come Racing!_ This is available from the British Horseracing Board and some sample quotes follow:

> The variety of horseracing on offer in Britain is unparalleled anywhere in the world and the 59 racecourses, each with its own particular character and atmosphere, offer a wide range of experiences and cater for all tastes and all pockets...
>
> The key to dressing for the races is not so much style as comfort: there's no point in looking terribly fashionable if you're freezing cold as the sun goes down. To enjoy a day's racing to the full may require a good deal of walking around, so give particular thought to your footwear...
>
> Aim to arrive about half an hour before the first race, to give yourself time to get to know the geography of the track and its facilities. Walking on the course itself, when allowed, is often fun and informative – and you will be given plenty of warning to get back to safety before the horses start thundering down on you!...

Your basic tool for a successful and informed day at the races is the racecard, your programme for the day, available around the racecourse for a small charge. (Do not buy a racecard from other than official sellers. A man who wanders up to you in the car park and offers to sell you one will have 'marked your card' with tips, and will expect to be paid well over face value for his insights!) The amount of information in the racecard varies from course to course, but wherever you are racing you will find it an invaluable aid to your day.

There is another stage of involvement in racing which does cost rather more money – but not necessarily a fortune. Just possibly (though for goodness' sake don't bank on it) a handsome profit could result.

You could own a racehorse!

The trick is to form a group of friends and establish multiple ownership. Perhaps the most famous example of this was the experience of six men who called themselves The Summit Partnership and jointly bought a horse called Earth Summit for £6,090 at the Doncaster bloodstock sales. It won the 1998 Martell Grand National and £335,998 prize money! In a partnership of 20 (the maximum number) that great horse would have cost just £305 each.

To explain how to become an owner in this way, the British Horseracing Board has produced another useful booklet, *The Thrill of Ownership*. But don't get carried away with what is undoubtedly an exciting proposition: as with the investment clubs we were discussing earlier, it's vital not to commit expenditure other than what's 'spare' from your foreseeable basic spending needs. And in the case of horse ownership, remember that you'll need to invest more money in the high costs of training and management on an animal that might never win a brass farthing in prize money.

So, if racing is to be one of your retirement occupations, have fun – but keep your shirt on.

Brought to Book

Superficially at least, there's probably no activity better suited to retirement than writing. Many people think they've 'got a book in them' or may well have been told so by their friends. ('You've had such an eventful life, you ought to write a book' is one of the commonest forms of flattery.)

You have time to plan it, research it and write it. Unless you labour under the gravest of handicaps, you're capable of sitting down and writing – or, at least, dictating. At the most basic level, it needn't cost you more than the paper it's written on and a ballpoint pen. However, as we shall see, prospective publishers will be much happier to take you on if you are able to present your manuscript on a disk or, at least, in typed form.

Mechanics apart, though, there are some key questions to ask yourself before embarking on the road to the bestseller that's going to make you rich and famous. For a start, have you something worthwhile to write about? You need to be ruthlessly self-critical about this. You must realize that what may have been exciting experiences for you – events that your family and friends enjoy your recounting – may just be rather ordinary to those who don't know you personally. If it's a novel you plan, then to replicate the success of a Jeffrey Archer, you must have a really gripping story to tell.

And, of course, you must be able to write intelligibly! There are those who would argue that the ability to spell or construct grammatical sentences is not a necessity nowadays, that the story is what matters and that spelling and grammar can easily be put right by the publisher's editor. And, it may be said, a computer's spell-check can save you any embarrassment (although it's unreliable at the best of times and may produce American spellings!). However, there's no doubting the fact that a well-written submission with a hint of style will be more likely to capture the interest of a potential publisher when you make your first submission.

You need to be realistic, too, in gauging your chances of success. In the world of book publishing, there is something like 100,000 new titles produced in the UK alone each year. There are more than 9,000 publishers. So you'll be fighting for a place in a very crowded market.

However, assuming that your optimism and determination to write is undimmed, despite my warnings, how should you set about writing for profit (and, importantly, for pleasure)?

Barry Turner, a most successful writer in a variety of fields ranging from newspapers to best-selling books, is editor of *The Writer's Handbook* (published annually by Macmillan) and he advises strongly against submitting your ideas and manuscripts to the top publishers. He points to the army of smaller publishers in the regions who are much more likely to consider your efforts with care and take the time to advise you on ways of improving your work if they think it shows possibilities.

In the beginning, Barry doubts the value of going to an agent, though his wonderfully comprehensive handbook lists a great many of them and gives sound advice on how to enlist an agent's help if you choose to seek it. This sentence, taken from the 1999 edition of *The Writer's Handbook*, seems to me eminently sensible, whoever you're sending your first efforts to: 'Write – don't telephone – to one agent at a time, sending a brief covering letter to the agent concerned. Too often, authors send photocopies addressed "Dear Sir/Madam" so it is obvious all the agents in this book are being approached at the same time. These go straight into an agent's bin.'

If you want to write a book, you should submit a synopsis of it (including the proposed length – say, 60,000 words) and the first one or two chapters, plus a brief description of yourself and your 'literary' experience – if any – in a stamped addressed envelope. I suppose the biggest challenge to the would-be writer is to sustain the original enthusiasm after the first few blunt rejection slips have dropped through the letterbox. But, if you really want to be a writer, that is almost certainly the initial price you will have to pay.

Some publishers – like Mills and Boon in the sphere of the romantic novel – are extremely helpful and go to the trouble of giving you a reason why your effort has failed to match their requirements. If your work shows promise, they may give you extra guidance about style or plot format or characterization, which will enable you either to rewrite or to tackle another story along their guidelines.

The same caring approach is taken by the editors of _The People's Friend_, a magazine in the popular romantic genre. The effort required to match their requirements may seem out of all proportion to the eventual rewards on publication (as little as £50 for a 3,000-word story, which you may have written and rewritten a dozen times). But don't underestimate such publications – they can open the door to a new retirement career for you.

There are more than 3,500 magazines published in the UK at the moment, hundreds of national and provincial newspapers and countless programmes on radio and television throughout the land, all of them hungry for fresh material by new writers. Clearly this book can't encompass all the advice you need to garner to develop writing as a profitable hobby. But here are a few relatively random thoughts that you may find useful:

▌ Read (or watch, or listen to) as many published examples of the kind of work you want to emulate as you possibly can, so that you become thoroughly familiar with the wants of the publisher/producer.

▌ Study the marketplace with the help of reference works, like _The Writer's Handbook_, so that you learn all the possible targets for your particular subjects.

▮ Present your scripts to publishers in the most user-friendly way possible – printed by computer or typewriter with wide margins on the left and double spacing between the lines.

▮ Don't fall into the trap of thinking that writing comes easy. It doesn't! Some of the world's finest writers, whose style is deceptively simple and apparently effortless, draft and redraft their prose many times before it begins to satisfy them.

▮ Tackling a major task like writing a book requires self-discipline if it's ever to reach a conclusion – and that is perhaps less easy in retirement as the urgency to earn a living from writing is missing. But you would do well to allot a specific number of hours each day to uninterrupted work, perhaps setting a target of 500 or 1,000 words a day.

▮ Dream, if you like, about making a fortune from your best-seller – but remember at the same time that the rewards can be extremely small. (For a book of 60,000 words, you'd be lucky, as a new author, to receive more than £1,000 in advance royalties and nothing at all after that unless it 'took off' in the bookshops. In other words, you might be better paid, in a strict financial sense, if you worked on the checkout at your local supermarket!)

▮ If you have a good idea for a radio or television programme, be extremely careful to protect your rights in it. The BBC acknowledges all submissions with a letter that explains quite starkly how many ideas it receives from countless writers – and how many of them may be coincidentally similar. The accident of two people having the same 'new' idea at the same time certainly occurs frequently. But it is also true that ideas are stolen by some unscrupulous producers (from respected broadcasting organizations as well as less well-known companies) and it is extremely difficult to prevent this. One way is to submit your script/synopsis to the broadcaster and at the same time send a copy of it addressed to yourself in a registered letter, which you leave unopened when it is delivered, thus securing your claim to copyright. This may seem a rather desperate means of protecting your rights, but you are venturing into a 'minefield'!

▌ Getting depressed about the whole idea? That wasn't the object of this section, so let's conclude with a fact that may stir you into fresh enthusiasm for finding the right market for your fulfilling retirement hobby. Dr David Hessayon, whose short and ever-so-simple gardening books I mentioned earlier, is now probably the biggest-selling non-fiction author in history. He is reputed to have earned £20 million from the worldwide sales of nearly 40 million little books.

So go on, get to work.

All in the Mind

The pace and pressures of life at the turn of the century have radically changed the way most people think about education. It's become a tool for building a career or, to put it another way, for making money. Look at the 'league tables', which newspapers and magazines are now fond of publishing, for universities and you'll find a significant proportion of points devoted to job placement after graduation.

But there are still many people – and in particular, retired people – who seek educational opportunities simply to pursue a joy of learning. Indeed, I suppose it's one of the great advantages of retirement that there's the luxury of free time to stimulate the mind for no other reason than pleasure.

Degrees and diplomas may add to the satisfaction, but they don't really matter any more. It can be said, at this stage of life, that if you choose to study any subject under the sun, you just can't fail because the only real yardstick is your personal satisfaction.

You can also learn new subjects – purely academic or practical, as you please – without getting out of bed! There are all manner of 'distance' or 'open' learning programmes available now to make studying at home perfectly feasible (though some would rather attend classes and lectures outside the home in order to enjoy the added bonuses of extending the social circle and making new friends).

And there is absolutely no limit to the variety of courses available, which range from learning to read and write on the Adult Literacy and Basic Skills Hotline, through computer training for disabled people with the Computability Centre, to gaining a place at a leading University.

You should be able to find details of all adult education courses and activities through your district library or local authority education office. Local museums and galleries also run special learning programmes. And there's a little-known organization, government funded, which is extremely helpful in answering any question you may have about learning opportunities. It's called Learning Direct and is well worth a call to help you find out about opportunities you never knew existed.

And then there's the Open University, which has regional offices all over the country. A call to them will elicit a pack of information about courses available, their length (typically, February to October), how to apply and their cost. As Chancellor Betty Boothroyd has put it, 'The Open University occupies a unique place in the academic world and in our national life. It offers the opportunity for higher education and thus for self-fulfilment to thousands of men and women of all ages and backgrounds who could not otherwise enjoy the privilege.'

Perhaps the most attractive aspect of the OU is the considerable freedom of choice, so that you can take the courses singly or put together several to build up a diploma, or a BA or BSc degree.

Foundation courses cover a whole range of subjects in the arts and sciences ranging from modern languages and the law to mathematics and health and social welfare. They cost just under £400. They may be all you need to enable you to pursue a new interest. If you do want to aim for a fully-fledged degree at the OU it will demand time and money. It's certainly not an easy option though, of course, it continues to be a wonderful boon to those who value the highest standards of education but for one reason or another can't attend a 'normal' university full-time for several consecutive years.

A complete degree could cost between £3,000 and £4,000. You're not automatically entitled to a grant towards these fees from local education authorities – but some of them do offer help at their discretion, so there's no harm in asking if you're limited to the basic pension and can't afford to pay for a course.

Many courses include BBC radio and television programmes. Others have cassettes as well as or instead of these programmes. The programmes are often broadcast at unsociable hours, so you'll need a video or audio cassette player if you want to record them.

Potential students with disabilities are assured: 'OU supported open learning is particularly likely to suit you if you have a disability, and we will help you to participate as fully as your circumstances allow in all aspects of study. For instance, we might arrange for you to have audio cassettes instead of printed course materials, or transcripts of broadcast programmes. Our services are adapted to your needs at residential school, in tutorials and examinations.'

A novel idea is the enticingly titled University of the Third Age, or U3A. It's what they call a 'learning cooperative of older people which enables members to share many educational, creative and leisure activities... a university in the original sense of the word: a collective of people devoted to learning.'

It was born in France a quarter of a century ago and has since developed its own English character with nearly 400 groups all over the UK from places as far apart as Abergavenny and York, Beaconsfield and Whitley Bay.

The official factsheet says:

> The U3As are democratic, self-funded, self-managed organizations that exist to provide daytime education and leisure activities for retired men and women at minimal cost. They draw upon the knowledge, experience and skills of their members to organize study and activity groups in accordance with the wishes of the membership.
>
> Between them the U3As offer over 150 subjects in such diverse fields as art, foreign languages, music, history, life sciences, literature, poetry, theatre-going, philosophy, world faiths, crafts, field studies, archaeology, bird-watching and computing.

One of the attractions of the movement is that it has no heavyweight administration in fancy offices with lavish expense accounts. Indeed, basic membership costs just £2 at the time of writing, which should hardly break the bank of even the most hard-pressed pensioner!

Although there are many groups around the country, there may still be none near you. In that case, the national office will note your name and address so that you can be informed when one is being set up in your area – or you might even take the initiative and start a local group yourself.

Let's Take a Break

After all the brainwork and concentration called for in the last few pages, you'll be thinking it's time for a break. So let's look at some of the opportunities open to you now that you have plenty of time to spare but possibly have to count the pennies.

To begin with, holiday planning in retirement calls for a completely new approach. You are no longer a slave to the pressures of the working years when you possibly had no option but to travel in peak periods. You can now wait for last-minute travel bargains to crop up. And, subject to what you can afford, you can stay away as long as you like.

In fact, you may find it even cheaper to take a long holiday abroad in the winter than it is to stay at home. This is because carriers and hoteliers are so anxious to fill seats and rooms that they'll practically give them away in the expectation of boosting their income through sales of gifts, food and drink.

One of the pioneers of the 'pensioner's holiday' was the late Harry Chandler of the Travel Club of Upminster who realized the opportunity presented by the fact that at the beginning and end of each holiday season, air carriers were flying from or returning to base completely empty. (These are known as 'positioning' or 'empty leg' flights.) He was able to offer free flights and almost-free hotel accommodation to pensioners during the winter months – the close season. And, as his main destination was Portugal's Algarve, people who took up his offer could still bank on a mild winter away from the worst rigours of Britain's fog and ice.

Nowadays, flights continue all the year round but the Travel Club is still able to offer special long-stay rates that can actually reduce your normal cost of living – as long as you don't spend every night in the bar. So it will certainly pay dividends to shop around for special deals like that. (Incidentally, many of us, when we reach the age of, say, 60, hate to be labelled 'senior citizens' or 'old-age pensioners'. We don't feel any older and, anyway, our pride is hurt. But pocket that pride if you want to find the best deals around.)

43

Of the bigger holiday companies, there's no doubt that Saga has earned a reputation for truly specialising in breaks for retired people. Indeed, their holidays are exclusively for people aged 50 and over and they have been market leaders for what the PR people like to call 'mature travellers' for nearly half a century.

Saga's special-interest holidays were referred to above in the section on walking. But there are many more. Painting, for example, offering the opportunity to capture beautiful scenery with the help of an experienced painting tutor; exploring some of the country's finest public and private gardens; all manner of crafts like calligraphy, creative embroidery, stained glass and floral art; indoor activities like whist and bridge; dancing, computers, bowls and even Scrabble!

'Themed' holidays are also a speciality of Warner, who provide what they call 'activity breaks' over a wide range including birdwatching, hot air ballooning, photography, health and beauty. They're all 'for adults only' so that may be attractive to those of you who still enjoy the company of younger people but would like a bit of a break from the roisterous grandchildren!

I suppose the holiday most frequently associated with retired people is the ocean-going cruise. It offers most of the pleasures you might seek: a whole range of options from doing absolutely nothing as you lounge in a deckchair to the more vigorous fun of deck quoits or swimming; probably the heartiest meals you're ever likely to eat; seeing the world with a new perspective and so much more. But a word of caution: however 'stabilized' a great liner may be these days, ships are still prone to rolling in heavy weather; wet decks can be dangerous if you're less than sure-footed and steps (or 'companionways') can present difficulties for the less-than-agile. Remember, too, that a cruise calling at many exotic ports may also require many medical precautions and visa applications before you leave shore. And finally there's the little matter of cost: The huge modern liners, for instance, offer a BB grade twin outside cabin for just over £3,000 per person for 12 nights. That's before you've bought a drink at the bar or disembarked anywhere for a tour. So the state pension won't quite run to that!

Flying can also be expensive. Round-the-world fares, which allow you to stop over at a variety of destinations right round the globe, are particularly good value but you still have to reckon in thousands when you calculate the cost of hotels, food and transport in your chosen locations. Much more modestly, you can take advantage of the fierce competition among the smaller airlines and fly to destinations like Nice or Rome for considerably less than the Shuttle fare from, say, Manchester to London. But, even with the very lowest fares, you'll still probably get a better deal by shopping around for an off-peak package deal. It's also worth keeping an eye on last-minute offers posted in travel agents' shop windows or on Teletext. You can jump at these offers and pack your case this afternoon. After so many working years of restricted holiday periods and the disciplines of a daily job, it may be difficult at first to get into the frame of mind that realizes time is your slave rather than your master. However, once you've done so, a whole new world of opportunities opens up.

If you can find the money from your own resources or a friendly bank manager, you might consider buying a holiday home in some sunny spot like Spain's Costa Blanca or the Portuguese Algarve. It needn't cost the earth and you might even make a profit on the enterprise – though you need to be extremely careful before committing yourself.

The best plan is to take a holiday in the area that appeals to you. While you're enjoying the break, travel around as much as you can to find out what sorts of properties are available; determine the market prices and costs like rates and public utilities. You'll get a better idea by talking to other owners (over a drink at the beach cafe, perhaps) rather than to hard-sell estate agents or property developers. Consider the possible risks – especially the political ones: buying a house in a country where rules on ownership, taxation, national origin and so on may easily be overturned is foolhardy.

Appoint a local lawyer who's familiar with regional and national practices – and who knows his or her way around the bureaucratic departments. Make sensible judgements about how frequently you'll use the house for your own purposes (remembering that scheduled flights are expensive), how often you think you'll realistically be able to let it (either privately to friends or through an agent) and how much you may have to pay for maintenance (of a pool, for instance).

The same sort of advice applies to buying a cabin cruiser (beware mooring charges and expensive maintenance) or even a caravan.

Incidentally, I mentioned right at the start of this book the thought of moving home. If you should consider the idea of going abroad to live permanently, then all the cautions I've spelled out with regard to holiday homes need to be multiplied a hundred times. You really will be in trouble if you 'burn your boats' in this way, only to find that you're not happy in what is an entirely different way of life. And think of what has happened in some countries as a result of political and social change.

Many years ago, a goodly number of British retired people chose to buy property in Malta, that delightful sun-blessed Mediterranean island which had such a happy and proud relationship with Britain. (It was awarded the George Cross in recognition of the heroism of its people during the Second World War when it was a vital naval base for our forces.) Those who bought property there after the war also benefited from an extremely low rate of income tax – a fact that led them to be nicknamed the 'Sixpenny Brits'. Altogether, it was a kind of paradise... until political change turned the dream into a nightmare and people who had revelled in their good fortune suddenly found their wealth decimated, with no redress and no way of 'escaping' back home.

Politics and economics apart, there's a vast difference between the joys of escaping, say, a British winter for a few weeks on holiday and living the rest of your life in a sunny land with no extremes of seasons. Having spent a full year (far from 10 or 20) abroad myself for professional reasons, I can testify to the fact that unbroken sunshine, with little more than occasional rain to break the weather pattern, can be exceedingly boring. And I developed a yearning, which started to become desperate, for the hedgerows and green fields of home – not to mention the people and the friendships that became ever more important.

Now I must not go 'over the top' in this matter of moving abroad. Many retired people have taken the big step and, years afterwards, remain happy to have done so. Just think about it. Carefully. That's all I'm saying.

But let's get back to the subject of holidays and a quite different option that could become a relatively cheap, and at the same time adventurous, way of enjoying your own country – which you've probably never had time to discover until now – and other parts of the world: caravanning and camping. In days gone by you might well have rejected this idea as being rather too rigorous and hair-shirted for your liking. After all, reaching the retirement years surely means that you've earned 'home comforts'. But enjoying the Great Outdoors in this fashion can mean living in style – thanks to the modern, sophisticated caravans, tents and motor caravans you can now buy or hire.

Helen Yendall of the Camping and Caravanning Club, which now boasts 150,000 members, says: 'It's an inexpensive hobby, offering freedom and flexibility. It is also a great way to make new friends. Campers (and our members in particular!) are a friendly bunch. We have special interest sections for those who enjoy photography or canoeing, for example, which provide an opportunity for members to get together with like-minded people. Camping is also ideal for dog and cat owners because they can take their pets on site with them – and many of our sites have fields set aside specially for dog-walking.'

For an activity that looks so 'physical' – braving the elements and all that – it is perhaps a paradox, but nevertheless true, that it offers special attractions to disabled people. The club has a fat file of case histories of people who are blind, or confined to a wheelchair or in many other ways disabled yet who are enthusiastic campers and caravanners.

Club magazine editor Peter Frost says: 'These are people whose horizons have been broadened, whose lives are renewed and enriched as a result of caravanning or camping. All of them have found that, despite their disabilities, they could still travel and go sightseeing and explore and enjoy outdoor life just like the rest of us. They value it just as much as any able-bodied person. More so, in fact, because their physical handicaps mean that they appreciate the experience much more acutely and enjoy it much more intensely.'

The club is particularly practical in the advice and information it provides – available sites at home and abroad, choosing equipment, security, travel services, even tips on saving VAT!

On Your Bike

Many of us have spent a disproportionate part of our lives driving a car – just to get to work and back. If we can afford it, a car takes on a new role as a pleasure-seeker in retirement, and that's an undoubted bonus. But is this the time to consider a different way of getting about, now that you're not in a particular hurry to get anywhere? In other words, have you thought of taking up cycling?

Consider some good reasons for taking to two wheels:

▌ cycling at least 20 miles a week can reduce the risk of coronary heart disease to less than half that for less active people;

▌ it's a 'green' form of transport;

▌ it's the cheapest way of getting about after walking;

▌ it's actually quicker than a car in busy city streets;

▌ you're not too old to learn, even if you're a pensioner who's never ridden before.

Publicity for the 1998 Hovis National Bike Week puts it rather well: 'The great thing about cycling is that it doesn't have to involve strenuous exercise. You can get fitter, going where you want to go, at your own pace, in your own time.

'Riding a bike is fast, cheap, easy to park, and provides real door-to-door travel. Even three half-hour rides a week will help you become fitter and feel younger. The regular exercise can make you feel less stressed, give you more zest for life.'

The cycling 'lobby' is a strong one. Several organizations will go to a lot of trouble to encourage you with basic help and information if you want to start cycling, like the Bicycle Association, the Cyclists' Touring Club or (and especially if you're also interested in cycling as a sport) the British Cycling Federation.

Most of us learnt to cycle when we were young and may have had Cycling Proficiency training at school. But if you've never been on a bike before in your life, many local councils can provide training and in London there's a privately run School of Cycling, which conducts evening and weekend classes for adults.

If you're looking for a new bike, the most likely type for you will be a mountain bike with gears, but take professional advice before you make a purchase because the correct riding position, giving you maximum comfort, is essential if you're going to enjoy cycling to the full.

Surprise, Surprise

And now (as we used to say in the early days of television magazine programmes) for something completely different. Because there are so many misconceptions about the sport, it may well come as a surprise to you that I recommend your considering croquet as a new – and, yes, exciting – retirement pursuit.

That is not because it's a game for old fogeys as you might imagine: one of its attractions is that it can provide an outdoor activity in which three generations of both sexes can play against each other on level terms.

The Croquet Association, based at the famous Hurling-ham Club in London, produces a great deal of helpful literature, which includes these comments:

> One of the problems of involvement with any minority sport is that few people know anything much about it and so cannot understand why it is so extraordinarily attractive to those who play it.
>
> In the croquet world the position is even worse than that. Most of the human race – in Britain at least – have heard of croquet and therefore believe that they know something about the game, whereas what they mostly have in mind when the word croquet is mentioned is a totally mythical world of crinolines, cucumber sandwiches and vicarage lawns. Oh yes, Lewis Carroll certainly has a lot to answer for!
>
> It is an ideal game for those looking for light exercise in the open air; it requires an active mind and enables the older groups to compete successfully against much younger players;

men and women can play against each other on equal terms
and tournaments are held throughout the country at which
players of various abilities may compete. A handicap system
is used, as in golf, to enable people of differing skills to play
each other.

As well as golf, there are elements of snooker and chess in
croquet. It's a dead-ball game like golf – so you're not called
on to display the fast reactions of a youngster to the fast pace
of games like tennis or cricket – and there's no need for
strong muscles, either. It's like snooker in the sense that the
ball has to be struck precisely with the mallet so that it hits
another ball (which may be up to 40 yards away) not only
at the right angle but also so that it ends up in the right
position for the following shot. And it's like chess in the way
that strategic thinking is demanded so that balls are placed
in such a way that they will affect the course of play many
shots later.

I've been surprised to discover that there are believed to
be between three and four hundred thousand people who
play some form of the game in Britain nowadays. Some of
them play the simple social version of garden croquet; others
play a 40-minute version of the game called golf croquet,
often as a stepping-stone to 'the real thing', Association
Croquet, which now seems to be increasing in popularity
all over the world.

Part of the fun of starting any sport, of course, is the
learning of it. And lessons are easy to come by through
croquet clubs all over the country. (The Croquet Association
will tell you where there's one in your locality.) At the start
of each season – which runs from April to November – there
are courses for beginners plus summer schools that provide
a mix of graded coaching and competitive play. These
courses usually last for a full week.

As in most activities reviewed in these pages, taking up
croquet can cost almost as little or as much as you like. In

the back garden, the cheapest 'fun' set will do. If you join a club, membership fees are very reasonable and the equipment is provided. Get hooked on the sport and you'll be shopping for your own mallet at £50 upwards – and possibly committing yourselves to travelling around the country, or even the world, as a keen competitor. As the Croquet Association points out, 'there is nothing to stop a septuagenarian of either sex becoming a county or even an international player'.

Oh, and it's not the vicious, cheating game that is sometimes portrayed. Or at least that's what they tell me.

On Course

It's not the purpose of this little book to state the obvious in reviewing activities that the reader may like to explore after retirement. So you may be surprised that I should devote a section to golf, which many would regard as the most obvious (boringly so?) older persons' recreation. Ah, but golf has quietly taken on a new dimension that offers a greater variety of interests, especially to those who find themselves with more time to spare.

I'll explain that in a moment. But first let's not lose sight of the many established advantages of the game:

▌ It's splendid exercise. I suppose a normal round will entail walking at least five miles, which has to be beneficial and especially so if you walk that far two or three times a week. Hilly courses are especially likely to keep the heart pumping. (Ignore that cynical gibe that a round of golf is a good walk spoiled.)

▌ You can play it competitively with almost anyone from semi-professional standard to the merest tyro – because the handicap system gives everybody an equal chance.

▌ Age and gender are no barriers.

▌ You can have a round on your own if you're feeling in solitary mood, or join up with others to make a social occasion. (Unlike cricket, say, you don't have to round up 21 other people to make a game of it.)

▌ The time it takes adds to its recreational value. When I first played a round, well into my 40s, I remember walking off the 18th green, looking at my watch for the first time since driving off, and being astonished that three and a half hours had elapsed without my having a thought for either work or domestic worries. In other words, my stress level had been reduced for a sustained period.

▌ It can be played in any weather. (No sitting for hours in a pavilion watching the rain come down and eventually abandoning the match. In golf you simply don your waterproofs and play on. I've even known people to play in the snow, using red balls.)

▌ You can play almost anywhere in the world, whenever you feel like it.

▌ Physical disability may be no bar: there are many fine one-armed golfers playing to the highest standards, as well as the blind and others with artificial limbs.

Now we can add to all those benefits some added interests like nature conservation, environmental care and new management techniques, which are being promoted in a modern approach to the game by, intriguingly, the Royal and Ancient Golf Club of St Andrews. In their book, _A Course for All Seasons_, it is written: 'One of the main delights of the game of golf is that it is played in such varied surroundings.

Over many centuries, courses have been successfully established in all manner of likely – and unlikely – places and it is a source of unending interest to play on them. However, a golf course is not an indestructible asset... Golf today is also strongly influenced by external factors. In recent years, we have become more aware of environmental issues and how they affect the game.'

In a companion video, Sir Michael Bonallack says: 'If you're playing golf, one of the joys of the game is that if you're playing badly, you actually have something else to look at! It's not like playing tennis. One tennis court looks like another. Golf isn't like that: every golf course has its own character and the character of many of the golf courses in Great Britain is the fact that you have wildlife all around you. Long may we keep that.'

All that modern concern with the additional factors of golf-course management – supported by millions of pounds spent by the Royal and Ancient on research and development of natural, environmentally friendly, well-managed courses – means that there's a new opportunity for club members in retirement to become involved themselves. You can play a part in identifying, protecting and conserving rare natural species on the course, or offer your experience from your working past in areas like environmental regulations, management techniques and so on.

Golf clubs will always remain 'amateur' havens in which captains and committees give time and energy to running affairs simply because they love the game. But today's world demands much more sophisticated management than it used to and if you have expertise to offer, and time to spare, you'll be an asset to any club at the same time as having an opportunity to expand your activities and interests in retirement.

Mind you, if you're not already a member of a club, you may find it difficult in some parts of the country – especially the south of England – to join one that doesn't boast a long waiting list. And there is a growing movement to try to reduce the average age of club players, which has been increasing markedly in recent years, so some clubs are reluctant to take on the over-50s as new members.

However, there are a number of private courses, developed during the 80s and 90s, which are very keen indeed to attract your custom. Some of them demanded extremely high joining fees in the first place, in the mistaken belief that golf was 'on a roll' and could command substantial payments from well-to-do people desperate to join. In fact, the market was saturated in some areas and new members were eagerly sought. Shop around and you may be pleasantly surprised.

Calling the World

Once upon a time a 'ham' was the popular name for an amateur radio 'freak'. Typical enthusiasts always seemed to be slightly manic, bearded men in sandals who liked to erect monstrous Heath Robinson contraptions in their back gardens.

But in the late twentieth century, the world of amateur radio – and television – has become a much more sophisticated one. It puts hundreds of thousands of people from all over the world in direct contact with each other every day and it offers a fascinating hobby to the retired man or woman who is not confined to listening or transmitting outside 'working hours'. It calls for no physical dexterity or exertion, the basic expertise can be easily learned and it needn't cost the earth (unless you get hooked on it and demand the latest, most sophisticated equipment).

If you want to know everything about amateur radio, you should get in touch with the Radio Society of Great Britain (RSGB), which will give you all the details – including the essential regulations – for pursuing the means of getting in touch with over one and a half million licensed amateur radio enthusiasts spread across virtually every country. The RSGB says:

> National, political and ethnic barriers are non-existent, thus promoting international friendship and understanding. Amateur radio represents a priceless freedom, which must be treasured.
>
> It is surely one of the attractions of amateur radio that it includes in its ranks kings, lords, senators, schoolboys, schoolgirls and old age pensioners – in fact, people from all backgrounds. Despite its long history, the field is still wide open for people to make a genuine contribution to the art of radio. The scale of operation by amateurs sometimes comes as a surprise. To date, there have been nearly thirty communication satellites put into orbit, built by amateurs.
>
> (RSGB, information literature, 1998)

Increasingly, amateurs are also learning to transmit colour television pictures to each other.

But before you dream of launching your own satellite, there is the little matter of learning how to transmit and receive radio messages. This involves a strict, but simple, learning curve that begins with acquiring a novice licence and taking a series of radio and electrical theory examinations. Courses for the Radio Amateurs' Examination – which will earn you a licence to transmit around the world – are run in technical colleges, evening institutes and local radio clubs nationwide. Your Regional Advisory Council for Technological Education will help if you can't find a course near your home. And don't be put off by words like 'technological'. All that's needed to turn yourself into a licensed radio amateur, they say, is 'enthusiasm and persistence'. These are, of course, qualities that anyone may possess and would-be amateurs who are housebound, bedridden or have hearing, sight or manipulation difficulties, should know that special arrangements can be made for taking these tests.

There's no need to worry about buying equipment in the first place. The courses mentioned above would provide all you need – and, anyway, it would be foolish to start spending money before you had a proper understanding of what you were buying. And, as in all fields of technical gear, there are some wonderful bargains to be found once you have entered this new world and met others who have equipment they want to dispose of at prices far below those in the catalogue lists.

As you gain more knowledge, too, you may want to design and build your own equipment. The RSGB says this is 'a vital part of the hobby. For some amateurs it is essential. The real fun for them is the designing and building. It is often the only way in which suitable equipment may be obtained – it may not be available commercially or built to high enough standards, nor at a price suitable for amateurs.'

Strictly for the Birds

As I write this book, it occurs to me that so many of the activities I'm suggesting hark back to childhood days – to interests that we developed at a very early age but had to 'put on the back burner' during all the years when work and parenthood left us with no time for time-hungry pursuits.

That must be true of many who look forward to retirement as a time to take up a youthful interest in birds (or ornithology if you prefer the fancy word).

I spoke to Bill Oddy, whose fame as one of the stars of _The Goodies_ has more recently been eclipsed by his TV series on birdwatching. I asked him – on your behalf – to explain the attraction of birdwatching and he found that difficult to answer, except to say that 'everybody notices birds and can't imagine a world without them'. Then he added: 'I suppose birds are the first contact most of us make with Nature when we're kids – being taken to the park to feed the ducks, watching out for robins in the Christmas snow, feeding the birds in the back garden . . .'

Whatever the reason or the wellspring of an interest in birds, it certainly attracts a lot of enthusiasts. The Royal Society for the Protection of Birds (RSPB) now boasts more than a million members, and many of them play a major role in its conservation work as well as just enjoying the pleasures of the hobby.

Bill Oddy's advice to people starting to take an interest in birdwatching after retirement is to 'go travelling'. In Britain there are the reserves run by the RSPB or the Wildfowl and Wetlands Trust. But there are also countless locations all over the world that you can visit under the auspices of specialist holiday companies with experienced guides or 'leaders'. (Bill told me of one man who took up the hobby after retirement: he became completely immersed in it, travelled all over the world and now has a job as a leader – so now his birdwatching holidays bring him an income to supplement his pension.)

The best sources of information about these trips are the magazines *Birdwatching* (especially for beginners) and *Bird Watch*. You don't have to worry about special clothing – 'anything sensible for the local climate' will do – and equipment is pretty basic: binoculars are essential and many people nowadays favour a lightweight telescope. When you're buying these, avoid the high-street chains and seek out specialists who can recommend the equipment that's right for you and your pocket.

Joining the RSPB brings a two-way bonus: your subscription helps the society to conserve wild birds and the places where they live; it also brings a wealth of advice and information and opportunities for seeing the birds. (Each year their nature reserves receive over a million visitors.) I quote from its 1998 handbook:

Birds are all around us and can be enjoyed in many ways. From listening to the dawn chorus on a spring morning to watching wild geese gathering to roost on a winter's afternoon or feeding the birds in your garden. To enjoy wild birds and the places where they live you do not need to be an expert or feel that you have to know the name of every bird that you see.

A good place to start is with a bird book and a pair of binoculars. The book will help you tell one bird from another and that will be the spur to further enquiry. After all, knowing what a bird is will always be the first step. You can drive along a motorway for years and see nothing, but once you learn that the quivering shape above the verge is a hovering kestrel hunting for prey in the short grass, it becomes difficult to pass a kestrel ever again without mentally noting what it is, what it's doing and why it's there.

Reach for the Stars

If the sky is full of birds every day to the delight of Bill Oddy, the sky at night has provided a lifetime's fascination for another television colleague of mine, Patrick Moore. Although his imagination was first fired by reading a book about the stars at the age of six, it's not too late to follow him when you're sixty. The British Astronomical Association (BAA) says: 'The contribution of retired people to amateur astronomy is certainly appreciable. Some come into astronomy as a new interest following retirement, whilst others find that at last they have the time they need to become really involved.'

One of the appealing aspects of astronomy is that amateurs who have made no serious scientific study of the subject can actually contribute to our knowledge of the heavens. As Patrick has written: 'No qualifications are needed to become an amateur astronomer, and it is quite true to say that astronomy is the one science in which the amateur can still carry out valuable research. In fact, the results of amateurs are widely used by professionals, even in this age of complicated technology.'

The BAA provides an example: 'The planet Jupiter has been visited by four space probes since 1973 but none of these could track the changes in its atmosphere for more than a few months. The Jupiter Section has watched the planet for a century without a break.' (The BAA is organized in sections that reflect members' special interests, like the Sun and Moon or Mercury and Venus or meteors or computing. An experienced director, who can give advice and suggest programmes of work, gather members' observations and even arrange for publication of their findings, supervises each section.)

It all sounds exciting, but where should you begin to develop an interest in astronomy? Patrick suggests that the first step is to 'do some reading and absorb the main facts'. So I suggest a good idea would be to read his own book, *Starting in Astronomy*. Then, he says, buy a pair of binoculars (for which the advice given earlier for birdwatchers is relevant). Buy an outline star map and go outdoors on clear nights and learn your way around the sky. And join the BAA or a local society, which will usually provide lectures by professional and amateur astronomers, film and slide shows, outings, social events and observing sessions.

Eventually, you'll no doubt want to acquire a telescope, but take your time about that. Even some of the outstanding astronomical discoveries have been made with the most basic aids. As the BAA points out: 'Comets have been discovered with binoculars and novae may be discovered with the unaided eye. The naked eye is invaluable for studying meteors and auroral displays.

'Nonetheless, the BAA recognizes that most amateurs want to make telescopic observations and, from its earliest days, has had an instrument loan scheme for its members. The largest mirror in the collection is an 18-inch but there are many smaller telescopes, both reflectors and refractors. Several hundred instruments and accessories now form the collection. Advance observing techniques are encouraged.'

Yes, but let's not run before we can skywalk. The Society for Popular Astronomy is probably the best starting point for beginners. It says: 'If you've an interest in the stars, you just can't beat getting outside and having a look for yourself. Despite the challenges of the British climate, if you wrap up warm you'll be rewarded with some splendid sights. All you need is a pair of eyes to begin observing right away.'

Well, you can't say that's beyond your means, can you?

Anyone for Bowls?

I've had a few surprises in putting together this book and my search for information about the game of bowls provided another.

I'd read that there was a movement afoot to change the image of an old person's sport and to encourage the view that it was a thrusting, modern game attracting all ages. Add to this my experience of other sporting governing bodies, who had fallen over themselves in their enthusiasm to promote their game, and I expected to be bowled over by the English Bowling Association's response to my questions.

Not a bit of it. It took me some time to find them because local clubs I approached said they were not aware of the EBA's phone number as bowls is organized in regions. However, I eventually found my way to their offices in Worthing and was told that the best they could do to help was to sell me a booklet, *Guidance for New Bowlers*, for 35p or let me see their annual report!

I was wondering about the wisdom of suggesting bowls as a pastime for retired people when I came across Jeff Applegate, who turned out to be an almost perfect role model for you.

Jeff took up the game when he was 50, took early retirement a year later, found bowls a consuming fresh interest, and had become secretary of the Buckinghamshire County Bowling Association by the time he was 55. He is, I suppose, a classic case of someone who can turn the opportunity to pursue a new activity into a full-blown occupation (with a token income to bolster his pension).

Jeff reckons the job – which is really a hobby – not only 'keeps the grey matter turning over' but offers a lot more besides: 'Comradeship was the most important attraction for me at first. Leaving all one's workmates meant a prospect of being quite lonely, but bowls solved that problem at a stroke. Playing in a match at the club is above all a social event. And, of course, you don't have to be a superfit sportsman to enjoy bowls, so it's ideal for older people.'

(Bowls has been trying very hard to become trendy and attractive to young people, though it didn't quite look the part when it was announced that the English championships were to be partly sponsored by a funeral-planning company! And Jeff told me that although his daughter had taken up the game, her enthusiasm was waning because she couldn't escape the conclusion that it's essentially an old people's sport.)

How to get started? Well, Jeff says you can 'just turn up' at a club near you and introduce yourself to members, many of whom will prove to be pensioners just like you. To join a club costs something between £50 and £80. You can then play free after you have been passed by an 'instructor' (who will be an amateur club member) as capable of delivering the woods reasonably and knowing the rules of the game, which are extremely simple.

If you enter for a club match, you can expect to pay an entrance fee of between £3 and £4, but that will bring you more than three hours' play – and afternoon tea afterwards! The season stretches from April to September outdoors, but many clubs provide indoor facilities on carpets during the rest of the year.

The only serious cost consideration is the initial outlay to set you up for years: perhaps £100 on a set of woods plus the cost of a pair of flat shoes and white slacks or skirt.

At the very top level of competitive bowls, the average age of international teams is now late twenties or early thirties – but there are leading players in their sixties, too, so there's room at the top for you.

Going, Going...

I have tried throughout these pages to concentrate on activities that are relatively inexpensive or even (like walking) cost nothing at all. So I was hesitant to introduce the subject of antique collecting, which sounds very expensive indeed – even foolhardy if you take it up without any real knowledge.

And then I met a man who delights in going to some street market with no more than £1 in his pocket – and spending the day eating and drinking in local cafes and pubs as he tours the stalls. Quite simply, he has a nose for a good deal. So he buys some old trinket, let's say, from one stallholder for his pound, identifies it as a piece with rather more worth and sells it on at a nice profit to a stall further up the market. He may do this several times in a morning. It's hardly antique dealing in the Sotheby's mould – but it's fun, it's practical learning and it's modestly profitable.

Similarly, almost everybody in the world of antiques whom I've asked to explain how to develop the hobby (which could be ideal for retirement years) has said things like: 'In the first place, visit auctions and antique fairs, jumble sales and even car boot sales. Listen and look. You'll find yourself getting the bug and then becoming gradually more skilful at buying cheap, selling for more – and keeping some things that you come to treasure for their own sake.'

This developing interest – and, hopefully, flair – will almost inevitably lead you to start reading and then perhaps to enrol on one of the many courses for beginners that night schools, colleges and some museums provide all over the country.

The next stage may be to join a regional club that caters for anybody who simply expresses an interest in antiques. However, as your interest grows, you may want to specialize. There are clubs for almost everything, from paperweights and blue pottery through ophthalmic antiques to textiles and even ephemera (paper collectables).

There seems to be no national body to administer or regulate the world of antiques but details of clubs you can join or events you can attend are regularly featured in the magazine *Antique Collecting* (published by the Antique Collectors Club Ltd). The glossy cover and some hugely valuable furniture in its pages may suggest that it's out of your league – but you don't have to buy anything to read about other people's treasures! And the classified advertising is pretty basic with useful notices about courses in subjects like restoration of pictures, clock dials and ceramics. As for items for sale, the issue I have in front of me offers a chest of drawers for £2,500 – but in the same column, a spoon for just £7! A purchase like that could be the beginning of a new hobby that could be rewarding in every sense.

Your Name in Lights?

To paraphrase an old Noel Coward ditty: 'Don't put your daughter on the stage, Mrs Worthington, but you might consider the idea for your own retirement.'

Before you turn the page to my next section, stay with me for a moment to consider an activity that doesn't necessarily call for your prancing around on a stage. Indeed, amateur drama and music societies cater for just about every interest and talent imaginable, combined with a great opportunity to make new friends and take on fresh challenges at little or no cost. And this is another activity that can be undertaken by those who are in some way disabled or less than fully fit.

Obviously, if you have (or think you have) ability as an actor or singer or musician, you'll be welcomed by your local thespians to audition for their next production. They're always looking for new faces and in my experience their easy informality and enthusiasm will quickly make you feel at home. Reading a part for a new play can make for a pleasant evening, even if you don't get the part. And in musical productions there's a lot of fun – and no disgrace – in failing to land the starring role but finding yourself in the chorus line.

However, if the idea of a stage appearance is your version of hell on earth, consider some of the many other options on offer in the world of amateur entertainment.

Wardrobe, for instance. Especially in period drama or musicals, there's a tremendous amount of absorbing and creative work to be done in researching the correct costumes, finding them in hire shops and elsewhere, altering them to fit and helping the cast to get into them 'on the night'. You can use your skills, or learn new ones, in the art of dress-making. And sometimes you may find that all this awakens a new fascination with learning about historical fashion.

Make-up is another key role in any production. This, too, calls for special skills that you may already have. If not, you can attain them by watching others who are expert in the art or by attending classes at a local college. (You'll find, incidentally, that involvement in the many roles connected with music and drama production gives you a fresh insight into the skills behind the television productions that you watch at home every day – which thereby greatly increases your depth of interest in them.)

If you're rather more technically minded, there are lots of important jobs concerned with the actual staging of a show – lighting, finding or building stage props, even something as simple as operating the curtains can give you the satisfaction of being part of a team creating a production that's both satisfying and fun for everybody.

But we haven't finished yet. There are innumerable jobs 'front of house' – selling tickets in the local community before the show and programmes or refreshments on the night, for instance. If you're interested in design and writing, there's the programme to be produced. There's a press and public relations job to be done, too – drumming up interest in a forthcoming production through the local paper and elsewhere.

It's quite a range of potentially new interests, isn't it? And you will have noticed that – as in most suggestions made in this book – there's no gender divide. I suppose women are more likely to favour roles like wardrobe and make-up, while set-building sounds more like a man's job. But it needn't be so and there's no reason why conventional roles shouldn't be reversed. In the world of music and drama you're unlikely to be met with raised eyebrows.

I Spy...

One of the myths about taking up a pastime that requires technical equipment is that it must cost a lot of money. That especially applies to the hobby of photography. Cameras, lenses, developing facilities can, it is true, cost the earth – and when you also encompass technical advances in digitalization, computers and video, the costs can be astronomical.

But hold your horses. It doesn't have to be like that. As the prestigious Royal Photographic Society (RPS) has it, 'Great photography isn't just a matter of good equipment and technique. It's more about the way you see the world.'

Or, more succinctly in the words of photographer Justin Dahinden, 'It is not the camera that counts, it is the eye.'

So, if you have an eye for pictures – from the beautiful to the bizarre – consider how you might pursue this extremely creative and challenging hobby without breaking the bank or exceeding your possibly very limited pension resources.

True, you do need a camera. But you're a very unusual household if you don't already possess one and if not, it would cost next to nothing to acquire a basic model – perhaps from a charity shop or even a jumble sale. If you want to become really proficient, so that you can enjoy the hobby to the full and make the most of the time now at your disposal, you might enrol for a City and Guilds course locally. This would certainly provide a detailed and thorough grounding in the basic skills of photography.

If you can afford it, joining the RPS would really set you up for years of pleasure and satisfaction. (The annual membership at the time of writing is £77, or for over-65s, £56. This covers the monthly *Photographic Journal*, which carries useful information about techniques, regional meetings, special events and, of course, some stunning photography that you'll find inspirational.)

The RPS also offers workshops on different aspects of the hobby including its popular two-day Absolute Beginners Workshop. There are special interest groups, too, covering subjects as diverse as archaeology and heritage, nature, travel, holography, film and video. As well as regular meetings, these groups hold exhibitions, run their own workshops and publish newsletters.

If you really get hooked, there's the opportunity to try for 'Distinctions', which are a very satisfying mark of your progress and allow you the pride of putting letters after your name. And it's an interesting aspect of photography that amateurs and professionals rub shoulders with each other quite easily at meetings. So, although you won't be thinking of turning pro, it's stimulating to find yourself joining in activities with the very best practitioners.

Going back to basics, another route for the beginner is to join a one-day beginners workshop run by the little-known Camera Club in a building that houses four fully-equipped darkrooms, a teaching area and a main studio. The snag is that there's only one club and it entails a trip to London if you want to benefit from what it has to offer. The beginners course covers basic principles like use of camera and exposure valuation; practical photography in the neighbouring streets and a nearby park; developing and printing your own film. You have to take your own camera with you, but otherwise everything's provided. The Camera Club says: 'No previous knowledge is required or assumed, but at the end of the day you will have produced your own black and white print from a photograph you have taken during the day.'

Perhaps it should be added that, despite my comment at the beginning that it needn't cost much to make a start in photography, there's a 'danger' that if the fascination of the pastime really begins to consume your waking hours, you will start to spend real money without much hope of return other than perhaps submitting the occasional picture to a newspaper or magazine that welcomes unsolicited work.

However, it occurs to me that if you were to develop an interest in moving pictures, like video shooting, there might just be a possibility of your developing a 'handy little earner'. I'm thinking especially of shooting weddings.

In recent years there has been a growing demand among those getting married for a truly 'moving' record of their nuptials and some thriving little businesses have developed to meet this. Potential clients are prepared, in my experience, to pay something like £500 for their wedding to be captured on video. They realize that that kind of money won't attract the professional television cameraman with his broadcast-quality camera and sound equipment, so they will accept

pictures shot on the ever cheaper and ever more impressive
domestic camcorders. They may even tolerate some rather
shaky hand-held shots. But if you were to learn the basic
skills in ways outlined above – and perhaps offer a professional a modest payment for passing on some tips of the
TV cameraman's art – you could acquire enough skill to offer
your services as a wedding video producer. (All of which
may get me into trouble from the professionals, but I'm
trying to be realistic.)

It could help your hobby to pay for itself and keep you
on your toes at the same time.

A Fishy Story

I was having a fierce argument some years ago with the late
Lord Hill (once upon a time famous as the Radio Doctor but
at this time Chairman of the BBC). It was all about which
sporting activity had the most relaxing and recreational
effect. I argued for golf on the basis (touched upon above)
that it provided stress-reducing exercise as well as taking
the mind away from working and domestic pressures for
three or four hours. He argued that it didn't compare with
fishing – and proposed to prove his case to me.

He took me to a private stretch of the delightful river
Kennet. I sensed the gods were on his side right from the
start because it was the most glorious August morning as
we arrived at that peaceful spot, the warm sun glinting on
the tinkling water and far removed from the noise pollution
of motorways and railways and aircraft lanes. I almost
conceded defeat before beginning to fish for the trout lurking
in those lovely waters.

I needed teaching, so Lord Hill took me through the skilful
routines of selecting a fly and (the difficult bit) casting. 'One...
two...' he'd whisper as he stood behind me and guided my
arm in gentle movements. After he'd decided that I had got

the knack of the basics, he wandered off upstream and left me to my own devices. I raised the rod behind me – and the hook got caught in a hedge. I tugged. Eventually the hook sprang free and embedded itself in my leg. I struggled to free it. I cursed – such language as I dare not repeat in a book for respectable senior citizens.

To cut a long story short, I became apoplectic with rage and more stressed than I could ever remember being. The whole experience was a disaster and I am definitely not the right person to be suggesting fishing as an activity to pursue after retirement. (I think I know what Samuel Johnson meant when he said, 'A fishing rod is a stick with a hook at one end and a fool at the other.')

However, I do acknowledge that there is another point of view. After all, there is something like two million anglers in Britain. It's our most popular participation sport. And it certainly has no age or sex barriers. So there must be something to commend it!

(And, if I'm to be fair, perhaps I should acknowledge that other famous quotation from the legendary Izaak Walton: 'God never did make a more calm, quiet, innocent recreation than angling.')

Coarse fishing, sea angling, game fishing, salmon fishing… the list of different types is almost endless. And so is the list of clubs and associations that look after the interests of their followers. So, assuming that you have had no knowledge of the sport in your youthful years, it's difficult to recommend a starting point if one of these pursuits sounds like your retirement dream.

Obviously, it would be a good idea to talk with (and, if they'll let you, join) friends who are already aficionados. Spend a cold moonlit night on a river bank or go into raging Scottish waters in your waders – or, yes, spend an idyllic summer's day beside a gentle river – and decide which is the branch of the sport that suits your personality and your pocket. (Fishing great rivers like the Tay will quickly eat into your pension.)

Then approach the relevant national association or federation for help in preparing and equipping yourself as a beginner. Visit the local library for 'a good book'. And, I suggest, read the *Angling Times*. This publication may fire your enthusiasm with its stories of record catches but it will also provide a wealth of tips from the experts (there's even an anglers' agony column!) and details of the best fishing spots to visit at each season of the year.

The paper is also extremely helpful in giving you guidance on the phone about where to seek specific help. 'Don't hesitate to call any time,' said a chirpy man at the editorial desk when I called. He almost persuaded me that I was wrong to draw conclusions from my experience on the Kennet.

Everybody Wins

Consider now an activity that can satisfy every special interest you may have; that can provide a new stimulus to your work-free years; that is of immense value to countless other people... all without a penny necessarily changing hands! This miracle recipe for a fulfilled and happy retirement may be acquired by working for charity, which is sometimes referred to as 'volunteering'. In one of their excellent information sheets, Help the Aged have put the case for volunteering simply and persuasively:

> Anyone can be a volunteer – we all have skills and talents that we can use to help other people. There are so many different things that you can do to help that there should be something to suit everybody! Many people get a lot of satisfaction from knowing that they are helping out and providing a service for free and it can be a good way to meet people and make new friends.
>
> If you decide that you'd like to be a volunteer, think about the kinds of things you like doing, and what you are good at.

For example, if you're a sociable person who likes group activities, you could help out in a day centre or club; if you're a careful driver, you might consider helping to transport people to hospital or on outings; or if you are particularly organized or good with money, you would probably be happy working in an office or on a local committee.

People often tend to equate the word 'pensioner' with 'old person'. To be politically correct, 'old age pensioners' are now called 'senior citizens' but we still tend to forget that there are thousands of people who have retired, voluntarily or not, on company or personal pensions, at the age of 50 or so. By no stretch of the imagination are they 'old' and most of them have plenty of physical energy and drive for decades to come. They can help old people rather than be one of them!

In my own town, we have a charity called People to Places that provides transport for the old, infirm and disabled. The idea is to help these people lead something nearer a 'normal' life by taking them to 'ordinary' places – shopping, perhaps, or the library, the pub, the cinema and so on. The full-time manager of this small organization is a retired policeman, the chairman of the management committee a retired banker, the drivers mostly pensioners. That's typical of charities all over the country, charities that need people like you. Some are able to pay expenses for things like travel and meals; others offer a small 'honorarium' to eke out your pension. All of them need you and what you specially have to offer, whether it's experience, specific skills or simply a willing pair of hands.

Many local charities work quietly with almost no publicity, so you may not be aware of their existence in your locality. But if you want to find out what opportunities for volunteering are available, ask at your neighbourhood library or Citizens Advice Bureau, or ring up the local newspaper and ask one of the editorial team.

If your community is a rural one, there's a relatively new opportunity provided by the National Lottery Millenium Commission, which provides funds for individuals or groups of no more than five. Grants are specifically for 'senior citizens' who want to establish activities for the benefit of people living in the country – activities like some I've mentioned in earlier pages (indoor sport, music and drama, that sort of thing). Awards range from £1,000 to £10,000 and the attractive thing about them is that they can cover all start-up and initial running costs – unlike many Lottery Fund awards which will fund only part of a project and require the rest to be found elsewhere.

If your special qualification happens to be the 'businessman's degree', an MBA, there may be a home for your charitable contribution in the Cranfield Trust. The trust offers free consultations to all manner of organizations needing management skills in the use of information technology, marketing, organizational structure, planning, budgeting, office layout and so on.

Originally, this scheme was launched to enlist the (unpaid) services of MBA graduates from the Cranfield School of Management. But now volunteers from other business schools or with other post-graduate qualifications are also welcome to apply. If they're accepted, they're placed on a register of volunteers so that the trust can respond to requests for help from charities by matching the individual's expertise with the charity's specific need.

We all have our priorities in responding to the endless appeals for help. Some have a particular fondness for animal welfare while others can't understand how that could take apparent precedence over humans. Some find the needs of children more compelling than those of the elderly. Then there's the disabled, the terminally ill, the starving millions overseas… Depressing as the scope of need may be, at least it offers limitless opportunity for those of us who look for worthwhile but stimulating activity after the working years. Choose something you're going to enjoy, using the skills you're lucky enough to possess. Then everybody wins.

The Good Fight?

As a young journalist, one of my first jobs (after being promoted from tea boy) was to sub-edit a delightful little magazine called *Field Sports*, produced in those days by a little printing firm in Idle, Yorkshire (opposite, would you believe, the Idle Working Men's Club!).

It was a labour of love that entailed reading contributions from people of all ranks who shared a passion for the countryside and its age-old sporting pursuits. From wealthy landowners to indigent foot followers, from molecatchers to kennelmaids, they pursued their pastime or their life's work.

Well, more recently, I decided to make contact with the British Field Sports Society to bring myself up to date with countryside affairs on your behalf, as they seemed a useful addition to our list of retirement activities. They responded swiftly and generously with an avalanche of literature. From it I learned that the BFSS had become part of the Countryside Alliance – and that I had ventured into a world of political passion.

One of the publications, *The March,* exhorted its readers to 'save the countryside. That means saving landscapes, saving jobs, saving businesses, values, communities and freedoms. Saving them from what? From destructive attitudes that are rife in the urban media and political elite.'

Goodness me, I'd stumbled into a war – a situation far removed from those gentle pieces about 'a day in the life of a falconer', which were the stuff of the old magazine of my days! I was about to abandon the idea of mentioning country sports in these pages when it occurred to me that you might feel that joining a campaign to 'save the countryside' might actually be something you'd consider well worth doing in retirement. So if it is, call the Countryside Alliance and they'll welcome your support with open arms.

Of course, it's still possible to enjoy these sports without getting involved in the political campaigning – and the Alliance provides some useful leaflets on many of them, like lurcher work, falconry, coursing, ferreting, stalking and so on. It's all good, basic advice like: 'Shooting provides an opportunity to enjoy the countryside, to meet new friends and to take part in an activity that requires a high level of skill. If you would like to start shooting, contact your local clay pigeon shooting school, or your local Countryside Alliance Regional Director and ask for details of shooting courses.'

There are lesser-known sports: 'Drag hunting is an exciting, non-competitive cross-country equestrian sport, guaranteed to provide a lot of galloping and jumping. Drag hound packs use foxhounds that are trained to hunt a man dragging an enhanced scent. The other form of drag hunting, often described as "hunting the clean boot", uses blood-hounds, which have a very keen scenting nose and follow the natural scent of a human runner.'

You'll notice I have been very careful to highlight sports that don't feature largely in the political argument: the debate about foxhunting, for example, is happily outside the scope of this book!

But, whichever side of the fence is yours, there are cert-ainly some country sports that can afford immense pleasure on those days when once you had to go to work.

A Crafty Idea

If there seems to have been rather a lot of emphasis on physical exertion and the great outdoors in these pages, let's now turn to gentler pursuits that can enliven your days when the weather or your personal circumstances preclude going out. Let's consider, for instance, arts and crafts. I suppose this group of hobbies has a rather fuddy-duddy image, but it needn't have. Indeed, it's become almost fashionable if all the associated television programmes are anything to go by.

If you're starting from scratch, with no experience of any craftwork, you'd be well advised to walk before you can run: find out whether this is really your cup of tea before you invest a lot of effort in it. Read some books, take an introductory course at your local technical college and then settle on a fairly unambitious project that you can complete fairly quickly. Once it's completed, you'll have a pretty good idea that this sort of hobby is not for you and you should turn elsewhere for satisfaction. Or you'll be hooked!

Actually, nowadays, a craft skill is less likely to be something you take up as a hobby; it is more likely to be something you 'get the hang of' while, say, decorating your home. There you are, seeking to create a fancy paint effect on the dining room wall – like that couple on TV the other night – and you become fascinated with the art of stencilling. Next day you're out shopping for a starter kit and a new hobby is born!

One of BBC television's best-known presenters in the world of arts and crafts is Caroline Righton, who told me:

> Crafts to be recommended are, for those without artistic bones, papier-mâché, decoupage and paper-making. These also have the added advantage of being very cheap to do. In fact, crafts in general can be practised for little or no money and often involve re-cycling and finding secondary uses for materials.
>
> If you are nimble-fingered, any of the needle skills are excellent and need little instruction. The great thing about a piece of needlecraft or embroidery is that it can make a wonderful gift that other generations will treasure – a sort of

heirloom. If you are unpractised at needlecraft but want to
have a go, then start with cross-stitch – it's dead easy – and
progress to needlepoint and then embroidery.

One of the crafts growing in popularity, I'm told, is rag rug
making, which is another example of Caroline's point about
re-cycling materials. I've been looking at a programme of
courses run at the famous Snape Maltings in Suffolk, which
introduces a 'rag rug workshop' (fee just £25 for the day) in
this way: 'Learn hooking and prodding as the easy basics
for your first rag rug. Re-cycle sweaters and skirts or use
oddments of new cotton fabrics. A fresh contemporary look
at an old utilitarian craft.' Throughout the summer at Snape
(and in other centres nationwide) there are inexpensive
courses, lasting from a day up to a week, on dozens of skills,
from all styles of painting to pottery and porcelain restoration, willow basketmaking, rushwork and chair seating.

Some crafts call for special equipment – a kiln for clay
modelling or a forge or soldering tools for metalwork, for
example. In such cases, you'd be well advised, for safety as
well as cost reasons, to take a technical-college course and
make use of their facilities before you make a commitment.

Although I've tended to characterize retirement as a
time of relaxed pleasure and stimulating challenge, it
does, of course, have its own worries and anxieties. So, the
undoubted therapeutic qualities of craftwork can make a
significant contribution to a happier lifestyle.

Caroline again: 'You will certainly meet like-minded
people if you experiment with craft as a hobby. It's a world
populated with enthusiasts. Don't be deterred by the purists
who say something can only be done in a certain way: it's
very trendy to be creative and expressive in your craft these
days and so what if you achieved a certain look with your
acrylic paints by breaking all the rules in their application?
You've just craftily allowed your individualism to break
through!'

Leisure by Numbers

Finally, in our survey of possible activities to pursue in retirement, I suppose we shouldn't ignore what is claimed to be 'the most popular group leisure activity in the UK, regularly played by more than three million adults'.

I mention it with some hesitation but I'm assured it is 'firmly established in the hearts and minds of the British people as an enjoyable and rewarding leisure pursuit. It is a sophisticated, comprehensive, entertainment experience enjoyed by a broad cross section of people, of all ages and backgrounds.'

That sounds rather like a piece of commercial marketing hype and I confess to taking it from some notes provided for me by one of the leading bingo companies. Add to that the fact that the pursuit is a form of gambling (shock, horror) and you will understand my coyness in bringing it into this book. But if so many people find it an enjoyable way to spend an afternoon or evening at relatively little cost, we ought at least to examine its credentials.

I well remember, several years ago, when I presented a late-night TV programme called *24 Hours*: we mounted an item about a government White Paper on gaming. The owner of a major London casino was invited to the studio along with a leading anti-gambling MP. We were about to go on air when the programme editor suddenly exclaimed: 'Gambling isn't just for wealthy toffs. Find me a bingo player!' And so, from the bingo hall down the road from the studios came a rather breathless and bemused woman who enjoyed her bingo evenings twice a week, spending just 50p a time. She proved to be the star of the show, very persuasively making her point that the game gave her a couple of evenings a week of great pleasure, some mild excitement, a social gathering where she made good friends – and all for a pound or two. It was all far removed from the big-time gambling, possible addiction and even alleged criminal overtones of the city casinos and it certainly couldn't be described in any sense as 'harmful' (except by those who believe that any form of gambling at all is wrong).

Since then, the gaming scene has continued to change. The image of numbers on ping-pong balls being 'called' in dingy former cinemas bears little relation to the high-tech environment of the modern game in venues that provide catering and other social facilities. I'm told that the average 'spend' for a full night out is £17 nationally, from which you can deduct a typical £6 or £7 in prizes.

Even the casino, they tell me, is no longer the preserve of the swinging moneyed set. Outside London, the average spend is just £20 a visit nowadays, which probably surprises you.

I'm certainly not suggesting that you might want to take up gambling as your principal leisure activity in retirement but the occasional flutter with a chance to make new friends could go on your shopping list of possible new pastimes.

3 Health

I approach this last section with a degree of trepidation. For a start, I'm not an outstanding example of physical excellence myself, being considerably overweight. And, of course, I'm not a doctor or even a healthcare specialist. However, I have picked up some sound advice along the long road through life and I have achieved a record of more than half a century of continuous employment without ever having taken a day off through illness. I have worked with many medics on professional assignments and I have practised recently what I'm now going to recommend to you – namely, taking the advice of the many public and charitable bodies that have published their researches into healthier, active lifestyles for people who have reached retirement age.

Perhaps, before we go into detail, I should confess my prejudices in this matter of good health. I believe that an enormous influence on physical wellbeing is mental attitude and that one of the most pernicious causes of ill health is hypochondria. We catch a cold and call it flu. We get a twinge in a joint and rush off to the doctor for arthritis pills. We worry ourselves sick.

Now here's a dilemma: one of the consequences of not having a job to go to five days a week is that, with 'time on our hands', we are more likely to become introverted, thinking and worrying needlessly about our state of health. Let's take a sensible approach and be aware of the ageing process and the problems it can bring. I believe that it's unhealthy to read too much about diseases and disabilities that come with old age – yet here I am suggesting that you read the following pages and, indeed, other literature that I'll be recommending along the way! I suppose what I'm trying to say is that you should be aware of how the body naturally ages – and learn how to delay or ameliorate the ageing processes so that you can maximize the pleasures of your later years.

Statistics can scare the life out of us – unless we interpret them optimistically. The charity Research into Ageing, which has done a great deal of excellent medical research 'for a healthy old age for all', puts my point precisely: 'Many older individuals suffer from a long-standing, debilitating illness that restricts mobility and independence, destroying quality of life in the retirement years. One in five 80+year-olds suffer from some form of dementia such as Alzheimer's disease... But four in five older people do not suffer from dementia, two in three have fair vision, four out of five are continent and two out of three women do not contract osteoporosis. These health conditions, therefore, although common, are not an inevitable part of the ageing process.'

That mention of Alzheimer's prompts me to give a typical example of the way people invest perfectly ordinary conditions with unfounded anxiety. 'My memory's failing – must be developing Alzheimer's' is a comment we've all heard often enough, and not always in jest. The simple fact is that forgetfulness _does_ increase with age – but that is certainly no sign of dementia. Indeed, the classic nature of that disease is that its victims aren't able to observe or analyse their own decline.

However, unless we take steps to keep it lively – for instance, by taking up some of the activities outlined in previous pages – the mind _can_ vegetate. (Oxford English Dictionary definition of vegetate: 'To live a merely physical life; to lead a dull, monotonous existence, devoid of intel-lectual activity or social intercourse; to live in dull retirement or seclusion.')

Saga have published a useful *Health Guide* by Dr Muir Gray (Unwin Paperbacks, 1998) in which the author stresses the importance of keeping the mind lively and staying involved: 'The best exercise for your mind is "mind wrestling" – talking, discussing and arguing with other people – and growing old and ageing are not by themselves major problems compared with isolation. Problems develop when the person is able to see and talk with fewer people than they could in times past because of disabling diseases such as arthritis. If you find that you are not going out so often either because of disability or because you are nervous of going out alone at night, try to find alternative ways of staying involved with people.' In other words, pursue some of the sociable activities I've outlined already!

I have a friend who religiously attacks *The Times* crossword every day without fail. He's rather good at it, having developed the 'cryptic' mind that it calls for. He claims that it keeps his mind active and alert. What he doesn't realize is that he's in danger of becoming a bore! Mental exercise shouldn't be repetitive: it should include variety and the stimulus of acquiring new skills, new interests.

The Enemy

Most of the following pages will concentrate on positive ways of increasing fitness levels and prolonging an active life. But first we ought to consider two negative influences that can have the opposite effect.

If you enjoy a smoke and a drink, you'll be tempted to skip the next few paragraphs because they make uncomfortable reading. I know this only too well from my own years of heavy smoking! But there really is no way of escaping the fact that cigarettes are likely to cause your premature death or, at best, painful illness.

However, the extent of addiction and the degree of pleasure that smoking brings makes it dreadfully difficult to give up. Arguments put forward by the 'anti-smoking lobby' (the sort of phrase that antagonizes the smoker) are too easily disregarded. We all have a 95-year-old uncle who's still enjoying life and smokes 20 a day – conveniently forgetting the other friends or relatives who have died of lung cancer or of heart disease. And it can even be argued that smoking helps to keep your weight down and so, in the tortuous reasoning of the desperate addict, it actually has a beneficial effect. It may seem incredible to non-smokers, but health warnings – particularly those in large type on the side of cigarette packets – have little effect on many inhalers.

The cost doesn't seem to be a great deterrent, either. I remember presenting a television commercial for the Health Education Authority that showed how people who stopped paying for cigarettes could afford to buy a flash car or an ocean-going yacht in no time at all. The effect of the message was negligible.

So how do we persuade ourselves that the immense willpower needed to give up must be brought into play? Perhaps there's a clue from a successful campaign that we ran for a time on the *Nationwide* TV programme, during which I remember a contribution from a woman viewer. She told how, one morning, she had gone into the kitchen to find a note written by her very young daughter. It read: 'Please Mummy stop smoking cos I love you.' Our viewer was taken aback to realize how her daughter feared she would lose her.

I'm sure that's the most persuasive argument of them all – the realization of how smoking can affect those you love. Your partner or your family or others who depend on you – are they less important than a fag?

Alcohol is a stealthier enemy. After all, it can be positively *good* for you! A glass of red wine each day is actually recommended by many doctors. However, it's dangerously easy to forget that they're not suggesting a bottle of wine every day. And don't try to kid yourself that a pint or two of beer is equally harmless, whatever your favourite brand. There really are significant differences between the low-alcohol variety, the 3.4 per cent light ales or lagers and the stronger tipples of 5 per cent and more.

In retirement, the attractions of the smoke or the tipple can easily become more compelling: The bottle in particular can become a 'companion' and drink can mask for a time some physical or mental health problems that ought to be treated.

In extreme cases, if drink gets the better of you (which may be difficult to recognize unless good friends drop a few hints) I'd recommend looking at a video, *One Day at a Time,* produced by Alcoholics Anonymous.

Here endeth the lesson by a one-time smoker and current drinker.

Now's the Time

You're relatively young, having taken early retirement. You're quite fit. No need yet to think about exercising to keep you mobile. Wrong!

Or you're getting on in years – into your 80s, perhaps. Moving around is becoming more difficult and you've had to give up some of the more physical activities that you once enjoyed. But it's too late to start exercising at your time of life. Wrong again.

The fact is that it's *never* too late. And it's *never* too soon. Today is the time to start exercising (or, harking back to the last section, to stop smoking: your lungs will start to clear from the day you give it up).

Consider these facts from the charity Research into Ageing:

Even healthy older people lose strength at some 1–2 per cent per year, and power (how fast you can exert your strength) may decline even faster at some 3–4 per cent a year. Without some form of exercise, muscle power and strength declines, making everyday tasks more difficult.

A recent study has shown that women aged 79–93, regularly exercising for a total of three hours per week, improved the strength of their thigh muscles by around 25 per cent in only 12 weeks. This is equivalent to a rejuvenation of strength of some 16–20 years. Another project showed dramatic improvement in balance, flexibility and strength in just eight weeks.

(Research into Ageing, information literature, 1998)

I find these figures nothing less than sensational – and compelling reasons for starting to exercise today.

But starting where? Well, if you haven't visited your doctor's surgery for some time, it would be a good idea to begin there, just to check that you don't have any condition that might make particular forms of exercise unwise. Then choose an activity that you will _enjoy_. We've looked at quite a few active pastimes in previous pages but the list was far from exhaustive: Tai Chi, swimming and curling come to mind as some we haven't mentioned in any detail.

For some, home is the best place to exercise. You can do it in your own time, at your own pace, to suit your own needs. But you should always find it enjoyable! You should start with modest goals, building up to the Health Education Authority's recommendation of 30 minutes of moderate exercise five times a week.

The best aid I've come across to get you started is a booklet, published in 1998 by Research into Ageing, entitled _Exercise for Healthy Ageing_ and written by Dr Dawn Skelton. This not only provides more than 50 specific exercises with graphic illustrations but also purveys some wonderfully basic advice on deep breathing and relaxation plus simple tips for a fitter life. For example: 'Rather than having a shower have a sit down wash using a flannel – reach down to your shoulder blades, reach up into the base of your back, reach behind your buttocks and the back of your neck. This will help increase your flexibility.'

In a sense, we can exercise all day long just by putting a bit more effort into everyday activities, from getting dressed (standing up rather than sitting down) to mowing the lawn or hoovering the carpet. When you're shopping, take the stairs rather than the escalator. Walk to the pub rather than drive if it's only a mile or two away.

If you're unable to cope with 'normal' exercise through some disability, seek the professional help of your doctor or physiotherapist to find an exercise programme, however modest, to suit your capabilities. Or you might contact an organization like Extend to find out where there are teachers in your area trained to give 'movement to music' classes to older or disabled people.

It's in Your Bones

Getting stiff? Finding it difficult to get out of that easy chair in the club bar after a round of golf? Not exactly leaping out of bed in the mornings like you used to? Not to worry – start the exercise regime along the lines suggested above and you should quickly feel the benefit. But there may be a need to take rather more care of yourself if these are signs of osteoporosis.

That's a long word for a simple but extremely common problem in later years. It means that your bones are getting thinner – and you ought to be doing something about it before the condition worsens and you land up in hospital. (There are more people today in NHS hospital beds suffering from hip fractures alone than there are those with breast cancer or heart attacks.)

We tend to forget that bones are alive and constantly being rebuilt. If you're over 30 (that's to say, any reader of this book!) your bones are getting thinner every day. You can't stop that process, but you can certainly alleviate it and minimize the chances of fractures and damage to your spine or hip or wrist in particular, or other bones like your pelvis or thigh. Incidentally, your chances of such damage are much greater if you're a woman – a risk factor as high as 50 per cent. Your doctor may prescribe hormone replacement therapy to give extra protection to your bones and there are tests available now which check any decline there may be in bone density.

So what's to be done to fight osteoporosis? There are three main things – an intelligent diet, the right kind of exercise and simple safety precautions.

We've already talked a good deal about exercise, but if you're an osteoporosis sufferer you need to be rather more selective about the forms you choose. Thus, while walking is ideal, but walking or running on uneven ground that causes jolting is not. Contact sports and those which involve sudden impact movements like tennis and aerobics should be avoided – but swimming is highly recommended because it builds general fitness to make walking and other movements easier, and it strengthens the back muscles which may have become weakened. Cycling is good for you and your bones – but only if you choose a bike with the right posture. Tear away on a racing bike and you'll cause more problems than you solve!

Indeed, posture is crucial whatever you're doing. It's as important when you're standing still or filling the kettle as it is when you're doing your morning exercises.

We'll discuss diet in more detail later, but specifically for osteoporosis sufferers it's vital to make sure that you have an adequate daily intake of calcium and Vitamin D. Think of it as feeding not your stomach but your bones. Calcium sources include dairy products (including skimmed milk, which actually contains more calcium than full-cream milk), tinned fish (like sardines and salmon) and broccoli or other dark green vegetables.

The need for vitamin D can be satisfied by seeking some sunlight, but remember to take the usual, proper precautions. Only a few minutes each day will be enough, but if you're going to be exposed for longer than that, make sure you use an adequate filter cream.

As for those safety precautions, one of the simplest is to wear sensible shoes. Women should avoid stilettos and high heels. (I once knew a physiotherapist who looked after athletes and had a display cabinet full of shoes, mostly women's. He would point to each shoe and testify to the spinal or other injuries it had caused – and that was to fit young bodies.)

If you have already reached the stage where your osteoporosis is diagnosed and your bone structure is delicate, you need to take other more basic precautions like removing 'hazards' in the home that could cause you to fall over and break a bone. But, hopefully, you'll be reading this before you reach that stage.

Not Your Problem?

I mentioned Alzheimer's disease, one of the commonest forms of dementia, earlier and you may think there's no place for it in this book for the simple (and sad) reason that if you become a victim of it, you won't realize it and can't do much about it. But it could happen to your partner – and if it did, the problem and the challenge would certainly be yours. You would, like it or not, become a carer – and coping with that role would be an inescapable, consuming part of life in retirement.

It so happens that my professional job has brought me into close contact with Alzheimer's in recent years and so I'm able to pass on some lessons of that experience.

I worked for many years with a cameraman called Pat. A top man at his job. Full of fun. In the prime of life.

And then… his work started to deteriorate. His pictures were even in soft focus. He became irritable and seemingly deaf when given instructions. Eventually I had the awful job of telling him that his work had become of such poor quality that I could no longer use his services. But he didn't seem to understand and soon became a pest, hanging around the office and even making a nuisance of himself at the weekends by walking into the homes of production assistants.

Finally, it was necessary to tell his wife that his behaviour had become unacceptable. Her shocked response was to tell me that he was acting 'very strangely recently – he's like a different person, not the Pat I've known for all our married years together.' It had all happened so quickly that none of us guessed he had developed Alzheimer's.

In Pat's case, the decline was swift. In many others, the disease takes a long time to develop and manifest itself. Audrey Brown's husband Stan had been a little forgetful and irritable, but nothing too much out of the ordinary, and when he was made redundant from his manager's job neither she nor anybody else had any idea that he was in the first stages of Alzheimer's. For the next 12 years Audrey had to care for a relentlessly deteriorating husband who could not even recognize his own son and had to be entertained every waking hour of every day. I met them and could only wonder at her physical and emotional stamina.

In her book, _A Matter of Timing_ (Book Guild), Audrey tries to describe what it's like to be a carer in these circumstances: 'Often, all I need to say is that being a carer is a difficult and tiring job. No more explanation is necessary and the questioner is satisfied. But not always. Sometimes I have to dig deep and search for the reality. I have to tell them of my mental and physical tiredness, of the emotional upheavals and the demands on all my reserves. I have to admit to the stress and the feeling of isolation. And I have to tell them of the anguish I feel as I watch the person I love go through the ever downward mental, physical, behavioural and personality changes which will ultimately be fatal.'

More famously, I suppose, there's John Bayley's most moving account of how this form of dementia overtook his wife Iris Murdoch. Neither fame nor a fine intellect is any protection against this relentless disease.

So if dementia befalls a loved one of yours in your retirement years, where can you look for help? Your doctor and the social services are there, of course, and some localities are lucky enough to have Alzheimer's and Dementia support services for this specific purpose. But perhaps the best source of information (which is what you need more than anything) may well be the Alzheimer's Disease Society. As well as useful literature, they have a video, *Looking at Alzheimer's*, an introduction to the disease and how it affects people's lives.

I hope all that hasn't depressed you – I know I began by saying this would be an 'optimistic' book – but Pat and Stan's wives rather wish with hindsight that as they looked forward to a happy retirement together with their husbands, they'd been better prepared for what was to come.

Feeling Low

How do you feel around four o'clock in the morning? If you're happy and well with a good sleeping pattern, there's no answer to that question. You've no idea how you feel because you're always fast asleep at that time.

But ask somebody who experiences Depression (with a capital D) and the answer may well be that it's the worst possible time of day, when even suicidal thoughts may arise, when the future seems to hold no promise but plenty of pain, when you hate yourself as a thoroughly nasty and unworthy piece of work.

At other, less traumatic times of day, the depressed person may feel an unexplained sadness – 'I don't know why, but I'm just feeling low'. One may be constantly tired but unable to sleep. Or bad-tempered, forgetful, constipated, suffering from persistent headaches that pills won't shift… the list of symptoms seems endless. Furthermore, the symptoms of depression are self-perpetuating because worry about health creates anxiety, which triggers pain, which increases anxiety – and so it goes on.

Of course, depression is by no means confined to older people. But it can be set in motion by the often abrupt change in lifestyle that retirement brings. (Something as simple as being offered a bus pass can start the shock waves!)

In days gone by you'd probably be told to 'pull yourself together'. Now there's a greater understanding that depression is a real illness and no fault of your own. Research indicates that it stems from the reduction in activity of some chemicals in brain cells. Certainly it calls for proper diagnosis by a doctor because it may have a specific cause, like Parkinson's disease, but as a rule it can be treated with the new antidepressants, which have a very good success ratio even if they usually take some weeks to become effective.

However, drugs are not the only answer and they may not be the best. You really _can_ help yourself by facing the problem as openly as possible. Instead of bottling up your feelings, share them with your partner or a close friend or your doctor. Face up to the things that may logically be causing you anxiety (as opposed to those groundless black thoughts in the middle of the night). It can also be a good idea to change your lifestyle by making it more interesting in some of the ways we've outlined earlier. More social contact will certainly help – though don't fall into the trap of thinking that 'going down to the pub to drown your sorrows' will help. In this condition, alcohol will almost certainly make matters worse.

If the root cause of your depression is psychological (and if you are able to recognize it as such) you might consider a few sessions with a properly qualified counsellor. Talking things through with a professional listener may bring something very simple to the surface.

Yes, it really could be a deep-down resistance to turning 60!

Making a Meal of It

The shelves of public libraries and bookshops continue to be weighed down by books about diet. Newspapers and magazines (particularly for women) are forever launching 'sensational' and, of course, 'new' diet plans to help us slim or keep fit or live longer. Some of them have a hidden motive – the public-relations-inspired promotion of a particular type of food. Some are based on a so-called breakthrough in food science. Some are rather dubious or even dangerous 'crash' diets of no lasting value. Many of them contradict each other with nutritional advice that has no basis in genuine research.

I don't want to join the queue of those vying for your attention in this field, but it may be useful to get back to basics in considering ways in which retired people can approach their eating habits. As the people from Research into Ageing explain: 'It is known that some 7 per cent of old people show some sign of malnutrition, and in addition, many more display symptoms of poor nutrition which often only become apparent when illness brings them to the attention of the medical services. Since poor nutrition is a relatively common and preventable cause of illness in later life, more research is needed in this field.'

Nevertheless, there are some incontrovertible simple facts that can help us all. For a start, all the experts agree that one of the most important ingredients of a sound and healthy diet is *variety*. Enjoying your food is the best key to unlock the body's metabolism ('the process in which nutritive material is built up into living matter' is my dictionary's definition). Now that's something which you can achieve much more easily than before because you have the time and the facilities of your own kitchen rather than the office canteen or the greasy spoon cafe next to the factory or the sandwich lunch pack.

If you're on your own or there are just the two of you, it's even easier to choose a wide variety of the things you like rather than having to restrict meals to the preferences of other people. Though, having said that, eating with friends from time to time can significantly add to the pleasures of eating.

You may well find that your tastes change. That's because the body itself is giving you the message that it has new priorities, which are governed both by the ageing process itself and by your new lifestyle. No two people are the same but the normal pattern at retirement is for less energy to be expended, while the body is less efficient in its use of some nutrients like iron and calcium.

Despite these changing conditions, the dietary rules to follow remain the same. You should try to have three meals a day – 'proper' meals, that is – breakfast, lunch and supper or dinner. These meals should together provide three groups of foods, each of which should be eaten three times a day:

Vegetables and fruit. Fresh vegetables, lightly cooked, are best but there's still good nutritional value in long-life items in the store cupboard if you can't get out for some reason. Canned fruit and vegetables, fruit juice and dried fruits, for instance, all have their value.
Carbohydrate. Potatoes (cooked any way you like), breads, oatcakes, rice and pasta – all in their many different forms.
Protein. Meat, fish, eggs, lentils, milk, yogurt and cheese – again in a limitless number of guises.

If you're a vegetarian, you'll have to be careful to ensure you have a proper iron intake. To learn more, the Vegetarian Society will come to your aid.

Drinking plenty of fluid – at least two pints a day – is essential. Water is especially good for you (and for your housekeeping budget if it's out of the tap!). It prevents dehydration – which can actually be caused, by the way, by drinking too much alcohol – and can even be a headache remedy. There is evidence that hard water also has the advantage of protecting against heart disease, so some experts advise you not to install water softeners.

One of the best pieces of advice I was ever given to ensure a long, healthy, active life was to 'work hard and keep your bowels open'. The first bit doesn't apply to the pensioner (maybe it should be revised to 'play hard'!) but care for the bowel is probably more important than ever in later years so fluids and fibres should be at the top of your list of daily requirements.

My own tip is a personal one that you probably won't find in any of the books. It is based on simple experience: take a brisk early-morning walk, then take your time enjoying a hearty breakfast. That will set your metabolism to work and have the effect of improving digestion and food-conversion for the other meals you'll eat later in the day.

Above all, keep it simple and don't let all those newspaper and magazine articles turn you into a neurotic dieter. In their leaflet *Healthy Eating*, the charity Help the Aged say: 'If you get used to missing meals, or eating unhealthily, you may start to feel tired, depressed and cold. Eating a good variety of food is important. If you eat well, you are likely to feel healthier, stay active for longer and protect yourself against illness.'

If for some reason your diet isn't providing the requisite amount of vitamins, then there may be good reason for taking some vitamin supplement. As a rule, taking vitamin pills each day can't do much harm even if you don't really need them, but there are instances where taking too many can be unwise so you should check with your doctor about your body's needs. (I used to argue incessantly with Barbara Cartland, the high priestess of vitamins and health foods, about the need for all the pills she swallowed every day. Her extraordinary longevity and energy seemed proof of their efficacy, though my theory was that heredity was the prime reason. I don't suppose we'll ever be sure who's right.)

Anyway, _bon appétit!_

Heart of the Matter

Heart attacks and heart failures don't just occur in older people. However, it's also true to say that heart disease and strokes are the major causes of death and of disability after the age of 60. So it's as well to be prepared – and, even more importantly, to avoid as far as possible the commonest causes of trouble.

The British Heart Foundation is the leading research charity and produces a stack of pamphlets with basic information, simply written. It has regional offices all over the UK and charity shops in most towns where the pamphlets are available free (though a donation is of course welcomed).

You could say that the wisest precaution is to be born into the right family! Heredity certainly is a major factor and, seriously, although you can obviously do nothing about choosing your antecedents, family history can be a most useful warning light. It should encourage you to take especial care about the other suspected contributors to the degenerative disease called atheroma, which accounts for a quarter of a million deaths from heart attacks and strokes in Britain every year.

Smoking certainly increases the likelihood of the disease. High blood pressure is a threat, which is why it's an almost automatic test when you visit the doctor with a whole range of different symptoms – and a key factor in taking out any insurance policies that require a health check. Another risk factor is a high level of cholesterol in the blood and the BHF say that 'probable' factors are eating too much fat, weighing too much, or taking too little exercise. There are other areas where research is less clear-cut in its findings – like stress. (I have tried to determine whether the increased rate of heartbeat caused by performing on stage or television is a valuable exercise like physical exertion or whether it's a dangerous form of stress – and I've never found a satisfactory answer!)

There have been wonderful advances in heart surgery in recent years – most of us know somebody who was at death's door until having a bypass operation and now strides through life with renewed zest and agility. Drugs, too, are giving a new and longer lease of life to thousands. But if you can, adopt a sensible lifestyle that may avoid either the surgeon's knife or the pharmacist's pills.

Joint Action

It was the simplest of accidents. I tripped going upstairs in an office building and hit my ankle on a steel-rimmed stair-runner. In no time at all the pain grew until I couldn't bear to walk on my right foot. Eventually I abandoned all hope of treating the injury at home with rest and bandages. My doctor gently examined the severely swollen ankle, which was giving me more pain than I'd ever known. He sent me for x-ray to determine whether the bone was actually broken.

At the hospital, the radiologist looked at the plates and announced: 'It's gout.'

I was furious. Didn't he realize that the pain came from an accident? Anyway, I don't normally drink port and the pain wasn't in my big toe. (My knowledge of gout was based exclusively on old wives' tales.)

In truth, of course, the radiologist was right. The trip on the stairs had been the *trigger*, which added me to the statistics of about eight million people in the UK affected by arthritis and rheumatic diseases. They're the most common causes of long-standing illness and account for a fifth of all visits to the doctor.

Arthritis in its 200-odd forms is by no means confined to older people. But its onset in the retirement years is common. Osteoarthritis, caused by the wearing away of the cartilage in the joint, mainly affects people aged 50 and upwards; rheumatoid arthritis, caused by the inflammation of the lining of the joints, occurs most commonly between the ages of 50 and 60. So we ought to look here at the best ways of fighting – or at least living with – arthritis in retirement.

As in most areas of life, understanding the problem makes it easier to cope with and probably the best way to start is to approach the Arthritis Research Campaign (ARC), which produces a mountain of literature on the subject, simply but comprehensively covered in words and pictures.

When you know the facts it's easier to develop the right mental approach, which the ARC recognizes as being most important:

> You should be philosophical about arthritis and respect it, but not give in to it or let it get on top of you… A positive and hopeful approach is half the battle, though this is easier said than done. Make every effort to make life fuller and more interesting than before. Your morale will drop after too much rest and inactivity, whereas hobbies and interests take your mind off your problems. Sleep is important – it is best not to take naps during the day but to save all your sleep for night-time, taking a painkiller last thing if necessary. If you have enjoyed vigorous activity and sport, you may have to develop less active pastimes, but there is no reason to let osteoarthritis get you down or stop you doing most everyday activities.
>
> (ARC, information literature, 1998)

From all the good advice proffered by the ARC, I've selected some key points for you:

▌ Visit your doctor as soon as the first signs of arthritis appear. All forms of the disease can be treated but your GP and therapists will have a better chance if they can start the treatment early.

▌ Painkillers don't treat the problem, they merely reduce (not 'kill') pain and may have side effects if you take unsuitable ones without a doctor's advice.

▌ Whatever you may read elsewhere, there are no miracle cures with diets. You can do more harm than good by experimenting with what you eat. Stick to the basics outlined earlier – though experience may teach you that there's an individual food that seems to exacerbate your problem. (I have found that grapefruit can trigger an attack of gout, which is otherwise dormant. But that doesn't mean that grapefruit has the same effect on anybody else.)

▌ Extra weight on ageing joints can certainly make matters worse, so if you're overweight it will help to lose some pounds – but not by crash diets, which aren't a permanent solution. Unless you are seriously overweight (when you should consult your GP) probably the simplest way to reduce that girth is to eat less fat, which may be the main reason why your body is taking in more energy than it's expending. If arthritis restricts your more vigorous activity, your body obviously needs less energy.

▌ Many forms of arthritis simply go away on their own. Don't bother to analyse why that has happened – the researchers themselves usually can't explain it. Just accept your luck!

One last thought culled from the ARC leaflets: 'There are many ways in which you can help yourself if you have arthritis. You need to respect the disease, but you also need to be positive about it. Do not let it get on top of you, or let it stop you doing the things you want to. Be determined to enjoy life as much as possible. Remember: A positive attitude helps arthritis.'

That's really been the theme of this book, so I'm not going to argue with it!

Health Checklist

Let's look now at a number of other health points which tend to be of particular concern to older people and which can reward sensible care during the retirement years.

Feet first. The enjoyment of practically all the activities we've reviewed in these pages is influenced to some degree by the state of our feet. So you're going to surrender a great deal of pleasure if you let minor foot troubles go untreated, developing into awkward and painful walking which in turn leads to all manner of more serious and even irreversible problems like spinal injury. Don't leave that bunion to its own devices: it will bite back.

I've been looking at a Help the Aged advice leaflet on fitter feet and it's astonishing how many problems are caused, quite simply, by shoes that don't fit – corns, calluses, ingrowing toenails and all the rest. Nowadays that should be less of a problem than it once was because the ubiquitous trainer or boat shoe tends to be softer, springy on the sole and altogether more comfortable than the 'formal' variety. (It also helps that the trainer has achieved fashionable status!) However, you still need to buy them with care. Make sure they fit properly both for length and width. Have your feet properly measured each time, because they do change shape as you get older. Make sure that there's no stitching or other rough patches inside the shoe. Obviously, if you're intending to do some 'serious' walking or rambling in the countryside, shoes that are not only well fitting and comfortable but also sturdy enough to be supportive and weatherproof are essential.

We've discussed the value of exercises already but it's worth noting here that specific foot exercises can lengthen their healthy 'lifespan'. Rise up and down on your tiptoes. Sit down and just waggle your toes around. Then rotate the foot from the ankle. All very simple but well worth the trouble. If you have a problem with poor circulation, massage can work wonders, but of course you need a partner for that!

Eyes. Over the years of presenting television programmes, I found that my ability to read the autocue (that's the device which gives the effect of rolling typed lines of script across the lens of the camera) was very gradually declining. In normal conditions my reading ability was still satisfactory without the aid of spectacles. But in the studio I became increasingly in need of 'turning up the contrast' of the projector or in some way altering the lighting. I didn't know it at the time, but I've since learned that people with 'normal' sight need twice as much light by the time they reach 40 as they did when they started work at around half that age. And by the time 60 is reached, the need is tripled.

That's just one example of how good eyesight is influenced by several factors other than simply focussing. General good health is most important. That's why you should see your GP for a check-up before rushing off to the optician's for a cheap-and-cheerful eye test.

Sight tests are much more than checks on what size of letters you can read at a specified distance. They reveal the health of the eyes – and that's important because early detection may make the difference between a cure and a permanent weakness. Once you're into the retirement years, a check every two years is recommended.

Incidentally, a good tip on taking eye tests is given in Dr Muir Gray's _Health Guide_, which I mentioned earlier:

> Ask the optician if you can try your old glasses on again after they have completed making up the right lenses for you in the special frames that are used during eye testing. What usually happens is that you take your glasses off, have your eyes tested, and at the end of the test you are able to see the test board clearly because of the combination of lenses that have been put into the special testing frame. The end result is obviously clearer than the blurred view of the letters on the chart that you had when the test started, but it is not necessarily much clearer than the view that you would get with your own spectacles on. So before leaving your seat, say to the optician, 'Now that you have prepared the new lenses for me I would just like to look through my old glasses to see if there is much of a difference'. If you notice a significant difference between your old glasses and the proposed new lenses, it is wise to have a new pair of glasses made up.

The most common conditions that imperil sight are: cataract, which is a clouding of the lens leading to blurred vision; macular degeneration, which leaves only peripheral vision and an inability to read or write; glaucoma, which is a kind of pressure on the optic nerve bringing gradual deterioration in sight over years.

Although much research still needs to be done to discover causes – particularly of macular degeneration – it is known that smoking 20 cigarettes a day doubles the risk of cataract and regular intake of four units of alcohol will also increase the risk.

Ears. It's quite likely that the joys of retirement may not be entirely unconfined as the ageing process continues. Hearing loss, for example, is something that can take the edge off some pleasures, like noisy social events. But don't worry too much about it – more than half the people over the age of 65 have a hearing loss. Are you one of them? Help the Aged have produced a checklist that may help you (however reluctantly) to answer that question:

■ Do you have to turn up the television or radio more than you used to, or does your family complain that the sound is too loud? (In my household it's the teenagers who have the volume turned up beyond pleasurable limits, but that's another thing!)

■ Do you wish sometimes people would speak clearly and stop mumbling?

■ Do you ever miss your name being called, for example, at the doctor's surgery?

■ Do you sometimes misunderstand what people say to you?

■ Do you find yourself asking people to repeat things?

■ Do you find it difficult to hear at social gatherings, in places of worship, or when there is some background noise?

■ Do you ever have difficulty hearing the doorbell or telephone?

Come on, be honest with yourself! It's sometimes humbling to admit the signs of ageing, especially if you're justifiably proud of your overall fitness. But it's important to recognize the signs and to do what you can to overcome them.

A visit to the doctor may reveal that your problem has a simple, curable cause. Most simply of all, perhaps, you could be handicapped by wax building up in your ears – which the nurse can easily clear with a warm-water squirter (forgive the technical language!). Or there may be some infection that will respond to antibiotics. You might be referred to a specialist if there are more serious symptoms. But as likely as not, the doctor will tell you that your hearing is declining in a natural, but inevitable, way and that you'll have to make the best of it.

Obviously, if the problem is becoming upsetting and hampering some of the activities you want to pursue in retirement, it may be time for a hearing aid. In that case, choose with care – and with as much knowledge as you can gather. (Some advertisements may lure you with false promises if you're ignorant of basic facts.) Voluntary organizations, of which the Royal National Institute for Deaf People is the biggest, are excellent sources of information.

However acute the problem becomes, remember there are always ways of fighting it, to make the most of all the other faculties you have. To take an extreme case, I remember watching a television producer friend of mine whose poor hearing was eventually lost altogether after an unfortunate operation. Jack (now Lord) Ashley, stone deaf, plunged into a new life of active politics, first in the House of Commons, where they gave him a special seat enabling him to watch the lips of most speakers, and then in the House of Lords. His way of beating deafness was to learn to lip-read.

There's almost certainly a lip-reading class available in your locality. It could be fun!

Cancers. None of us can claim that we're not scared by the word 'cancer' – the 'Big C' as the more emotional would call it. It has struck twice in my own family so I'm only too familiar with its terrors. In our cases, cures were achieved. Many types of the disease are now treatable – but that doesn't really lessen the fear. Older men particularly seem to worry about prostate cancer; women are concerned about the fact that cervical smears and breast check-ups may not be available on the NHS when they get older; both men and women may fear cancer of the colon but are often too embarrassed to seek advice if there are changes in their bowel habits.

In all these and other areas of cancer risk, be sensible. Don't keep any worries to yourself – consult your doctor right away. Delay could have serious consequences. There are additional ways of seeking information that can often calm your fears. For a start there are now many cancer charities which provide literature and respond most warmly to any enquiries you may make over the telephone. And we've found the Internet a wonderful source. Ask it for information on any aspect of cancer and you'll have enough reading for days on end!

Sex. A woman said to me the other day: 'Since my husband and I both retired, we're having the best sex of our lives!' And in that simple statement, it seemed to me, there was a lot of worldly wisdom. To begin with, it emphasizes the point that our sexual appetites and pleasures need never decline. Advancing age, of itself, is no threat to sexual activity. Certainly a man will not have the physical vigour that he had when he was 16 – but his potency should remain all his life, and a couple's pleasure should actually increase with experienced technique.

It's reported that something like 10 per cent of all adult men suffer from impotency. But that has nothing to do with age: a variety of illnesses, or too much alcohol, or (particularly likely) psychological factors may be the reason.

There's time now, in retirement, to enjoy sex unhindered by the pressures of working hours, bringing up a family and suchlike.

And don't rush to the Viagra tablets if your libido seems to be waning or your 'performance' seems to be in decline. If there really is a problem that can't be resolved by talking about it together, visit your GP – who may refer you to a specialist if necessary. You'll almost certainly discover that any problem you have will not be due to old age.

Skin. I suppose men, as a rule, don't care too much about the state of their skin. Wrinkles, so-called 'liver spots' on the back of the hands, lines round the eyes... they don't hamper normal activity, so why worry about them? Ah, but women *do* have a care for these things!

Not that there's a great deal you can do, when you're retired, to repair whatever damage you may have done in years gone by. The most telling factor by far is exposure to the sun – and if you spent a lot of time in your younger days maintaining a 'healthy' (which was really an *un*healthy) tan, there's not much you can do about its effects now other than avoiding too much sunlight and applying moisturizers.

If you can afford it (and you certainly can't on a basic pension) you might be tempted to seek a facelift or some other cosmetic surgical treatment. If you do, be very careful. The world of cosmetic surgery is full of 'cowboys' operating from 'clinics' without proper qualifications. Their work can go wrong and cause awful problems that may be irreversible. So you *must* consult your GP first (a recurring theme in this book). If he or she sees no reason why you shouldn't have surgery, ask to be referred to a member of the British Association of Aesthetic Plastic Surgeons, all of whose members are not only Fellows of the Royal College but also have years of specialized experience in this work.

You have been warned…

You and Your Doctor

One last thought on the subject of health. It was prompted by a conversation with Christine Doyle of the *Daily Telegraph* who pointed out how important it is to be able to communicate with – indeed, make a friend of – your doctor. 'Many people', she said, 'are still incredibly awed by doctors and feel tongue-tied and servile in the surgery. Some of your readers – men more than women – may not have been to the doc often but are now entering the risky age range so it's important that they learn to give the doctor a chance to understand their needs.'

If ever I visit the doctor's surgery I find myself in the comical situation arising from a conversation that goes something like this:

'Morning, doctor, how are you?'

'Fine, thanks. And you?'

'Yes, very well, thank you.' At which point I half expect him to ask me why, if that's the case, I'm wasting his time!

Seriously, though, it really is important to brush up your communication skills in the surgery. I think it's a good idea to make out a 'shopping list' before you go, noting the various causes of your concern and the symptoms that may help him in his diagnosis. Without such a list, it's so easy to forget something that may (for all you know) be quite important – and so annoying to remember it afterwards!

Ask questions – again, a list of the things you want to know will be useful – but don't try to provide your own answers. In other words, don't annoy the doctor by suggesting some diagnosis or remedy based on what you've been reading in the health column in your newspaper or magazine.

Keep that notebook handy to jot down the things you're told.

Try to talk to him or her as a friend you trust. That will help to create the kind of good relationship that's such a vital ingredient of effective communication between the two of you.

Don't be worried about making a fool of yourself. We all have groundless fears from time to time of some phantom illness and we won't rid ourselves of them unless we bring them out in the open. Anyway, sometimes it's *not* a phantom.

The good relationship we're trying to encourage will enable you to ask for a second opinion if you still have any doubts after a consultation. There is no reason whatsoever why you shouldn't do this and the doctor certainly won't think any the worse of you.

I'm also aware, of course, that good communication is a two-way process and, in this respect, there's a heavy responsibility on the doctor, too. In the past there has been far too little training of medical staff in how to converse effectively with patients. Now that's beginning to change and there's much greater emphasis on the 'duty to inform'.

In a word, the art of communication is the art of _listening_. If you and your doctor listen to each other, you'll both be better for it!

In Conclusion

The last few pages seem to have dwelt on some possibly depressing features of the third stage in life – declining faculties, brittle bones, that sort of thing – but I hope you've derived from them nevertheless an optimistic message. We'd be daft to ignore the inevitability of ageing but we can still make the most of what we have by taking positive steps to safeguard and even improve our health.

You may think that most of the advice has been so basic that it hardly needed stating. Eat more sensibly? Exercise to keep fit? Big deal! But even with 50 or 60 years' experience under our belt, most of us tend to forget, or ignore, the simple things that make life better.

My own belief as a professional observer of human behaviour is that _attitude_ is the key. Positive thinking can overcome so many physical hurdles; new interests can add a whole new dimension to the post-retirement years and turn them into a real bonus.

The one essential ingredient of a personal plan to make the most of retirement is knowledge. You need to know where to turn for the information that will enable you to maximize your enjoyment of each day. So the following pages include details of how to contact organizations available to help you. Some of them are public bodies whose services you've helped to pay for throughout your working life, so don't be coy about making full use of them now! Others are charities, many of which I have found particularly helpful in collecting information for this book. (Most of them would value your help, too!)

Go to it!

Appendix:
Useful Addresses

Action on Smoking and Health (ASH), 109 Gloucester Place, London W1H 4EJ (tel: 0171 935 3519)

Age Concern England, Astral House, 1268 London Road, London SW16 4ER (tel: 0181 679 8000)

Age-Link, Narborough Close, Brackenbury Village, Ickenham, Middx UB10 8TN (tel: 0181 571 5888)

Alzheimer's Disease Society, Gordon House, 10 Greencoat Place, London SW1P 1PH (tel: 0171 306 0606)

Angling Times, Bushfield House, Orton Centre, Peterborough PE5 5UW (tel: 01733 266222)

Antique Collectors Club, 5 Church Street, Woodbridge, Suffolk IP12 1DS (tel: 01394 385501)

Arthritis Care, 18 Stephenson Way, London NW1 2HD (freefone helpline 0800 289 170)

Arthritis Research Campaign, St Mary's Gate, Chesterfield, Derbyshire S41 STD (tel: 01246 558033)

Association of British Credit Unions, Unit 307, Westminster Business Square, 339 Kennington Lane, London SE11 5QY (tel: 0171 582 2626)

Association of British Insurers, 51 Gresham Street, London EC2V 7HQ (tel: 0171 600 3333)

Banking Information Service, Pinners Hall, 105–108 Old Broad Street, London EC2N 1EX

Bicycle Association, Starley House, Eaton Road, Coventry CV1 2FH (tel: 01203 553838)

Birmingham Settlement ('National Debtline': helpline for people with money problems; tel: 0121 359 8501)

British Association for Local History, Shopwyke Hall, Chichester, West Sussex PO20 6BQ (tel: 01234 787639)

British Astronomical Association, Burlington House, Piccadilly, London W1V 0NL (tel: 0171 734 4145)

British Horseracing Board, 42 Portman Square, London W1H 0EN (tel: 0171 396 0011)

British Red Cross Society, 9 Grosvenor Crescent, London SW1X 7EJ (tel: 0171 235 5454)

Camera Club, 16 Bowden Street, London SE11 4DS (tel: 0171 587 1809)

Camping and Caravanning Club, Greenfields House, Westwood Way, Coventry CV4 8JH (tel: 01203 694886)

Cancer BACUP, 3 Bath Place, Rivington Street, London EC2A 3JR (freefone helpline: 0800 181199)

Carers National Association, 20–25 Glasshouse Yard, London EC1A 4JS (helpline: 0345 573369)

Central Council for Physical Recreation, Francis House, Francis Street, London SW1P 1DE (tel: 0171 828 3163)

City and Guilds of London Institute, 1 Giltspur Street, London EC1A 9DD (tel: 0171 294 2468)

Contact the Elderly, 15 Henrietta Street, London WC2E 8QH (tel: 0171 240 0630)

Country Venture Activities, The Old School, Tebay, Cumbria CA10 3TP (tel: 015396 24286)

Countryside Alliance, The Old Town Hall, 367 Kennington Road, London SE11 4PT (tel: 0171 582 5432)

Cranfield Trust, Blue Gates Farm, Ashwell End, Baldock, Herts. (tel: 01462 743022)

Croquet Association, c/o The Hurlingham Club, Ranelagh Gardens, London SW6 3PR (tel: 0171 736 3148)

CTC (Cyclists' Touring Club), Cotterell House, 69 Meadrow, Godalming, Surrey GU7 3HS (tel: 01483 417217)

Disabled Living Foundation, 380–384 Harrow Road, London W9 2HU (helpline: 0870 603 9177)

Embroiderers Guild, Apt 41a Hampton Court Palace, East Molesey, Surrey (tel: 0181 943 1229)

English Bowling Association, 2a Iddesleigh Road, Bourne-mouth, Hants.

Extend, 22 Maltings Drive, Wheathampstead, Herts. AL4 8QJ (tel: 01582 832760)

Eyecare Information Service, PO Box 3597, London SE1 6DY (tel: 0171 357 7730)

Glenmore Lodge Outdoor Centre, Aviemore, Invernesshire PH22 1QU (tel: 01479 861276)

Health Education Authority, Trevelyan House, 30 Great Peter Street, London SW1P 2HW (tel: 0171 222 5300)

Hearing Aid Council, Witan Court, 305 Upper Fourth Street, Milton Keynes MK9 1EH (tel: 01908 235700)

Hearing Concern, 7–11 Armstrong Road, London W3 7JL (tel: 0181 743 1110)

Help the Aged, St James's Walk, London EC1R 0BE (Senior Line, free national information service for senior citizens, their relatives, carers and friends: 0800 650 065)

Holiday Care Service, 2nd Floor, Imperial Buildings, Victoria Road, Horley, Surrey RH6 7PZ (tel: 01293 774535)

Horticultural Therapy, Goulds Ground, Vallis Way, Frome, Somerset BA11 3DW (tel: 01373 464782)

Inland Revenue Public Enquiry Office, Somerset House, The Strand, London WC2R 1LB (tel: 0171 438 6420)

Inland Waterways Association, 114 Regent's Park Road, London NW1 8UQ (tel: 0171 586 2510)

Keep Fit Association, Francis House, Francis Street, London SW1P 1DE (tel: 0171 233 8898)

Learning Direct (freefone: 0800 100900)

London School of Tai Chi Chuan and Traditional Health Resources, PO Box 9836, London SE3 0ZG

London Stock Exchange, Public Affairs Department, Old Broad Street, London EC2N 1HP (tel: 0171 588 2355)

National Adult School Association, MASU Centre, Gaywood Croft, Cregoe Street, Birmingham B15 2ED

National Association of Volunteer Bureaux, New Oxford House, 16 Waterloo Street, Birmingham B2 5UG (tel: 0121 633 4555)

National Backpain Association, The Old Office Block, Elstree Road, Teddington, Middx TW11 8JT (tel: 0181 977 5474)

National Federation of Music Societies, Francis House, Francis Stree,t London SW1P 1DE (tel: 0171 828 7320)

National Mountain Centre, Plas y Brenin, Capel Curig, Gwynedd LL24 0ET (tel: 01690 720214)

National Osteoporosis Society, PO Box 10, Radstock, Bath BA3 3YB (tel: 01761 471771)

National Society of Allotment and Leisure Gardeners, O'Dell House, Hunters Road, Corby, Northamptonshire NN17 1JE

NPI In-retirement Services, 30–36 Newport Road, Cardiff CF2 1DE (tel: 01222 782360)

Open and Distance Learning Quality Council, 27 Marylebone Road, London NW1 5JS (tel: 0171 935 5391)

Open College of The Arts, Houndhill, Worsbrough, Barnsley, South Yorkshire S70 6TU (tel: 01226 730495)

Open University, PO Box 724, Milton Keynes MK7 6ZS (tel: 01908 653231)

Parkinson's Disease Society, 22 Upper Woburn Place, London WCI (helpline: 0171 388 5798)

Peak National Park Centre, Losehill Hall, Castleton, Derbys S30 2WB (tel: 01433 620373)

Personal Investment Authority (PIA), 7th Floor, 1 Canada Square, London E14 5AZ (tel: 0171 538 8860)

ProShare, Library Chambers, 13–14 Basinghall Street, London EC2V 5BQ (tel: 0171 600 0984)

Radio Society of Great Britain, Lambda House, Cranborne Road, Potters Bar, Herts. EN6 3JE (tel: 01707 659015)

Ramblers' Association, 1–5 Wandsworth Road, London SW8 2XX (tel: 0171 339 8500)

Research into Ageing, 15–17 St Cross Street, London EC1N 8UN (tel: 0171 404 6878)

Retired Executives Action Clearing House (REACH), Bear Wharf, 27 Bankside, London SE1 9ET (tel: 0171 928 0452)

Retired Senior Volunteer Programme (RSVP), 237 Pentonville Road, London N1 9NJ (tel: 0171 278 6601)

Royal Horticultural Society, PO Box 313, London SW1 (tel: 0171 834 4333)

Royal National Institute for Deaf People (RNID), 19–23 Featherstone Street, London EC1Y 8SL (tel: 0171 296 8000)

Royal National Institute for the Blind (RNIB), 224 Great Portland Street, London W1 (tel: 0171 388 1266)

Royal Photographic Society of Great Britain, The Octagon, Milson Street, Bath BA1 1DN (tel: 01225 462841)

Royal Society for the Protection of Birds (RSPB), The Lodge, Sandy, Bedfordshire SG19 2DL (tel: 01767 680551)

Running Sixties, 120 Norfolk Avenue, Sanderstead, Surrey CR2 8BS (tel: 0181 657 7660)

Saga Group, Saga Building, Middleburg Square, Folkestone, Kent CT20 1AZ (tel: 01303 711111)

Scottish Youth Hostels Association, 7 Glebe Crescent, Stirling FK8 2JA (tel: 01786 451181)

Society of Authors, 84 Drayton Gardens, London SW10 9SB (tel: 0171 373 6642)

Spinal Injuries Association, Newpoint House, 76 St James's Lane, London N10 3DF (tel: 0181 444 2121)

Sports Council, 16 Upper Woburn Place, London WC1H 0QP (tel: 0171 388 1277)

Third Age Challenge, Anglia House, 115 Commercial Road, Swindon SN1 5PL

Third Age Network, Friary Mews, 28 Commercial Road, Guildford, Surrey GU1 4SU (tel: 01483 440582)

Travel Club of Upminster, Station Road, Upminster, Essex RM14 2TT (tel: 01708 223000)

University of the Third Age, 26 Harrison Street, London WC1H 8JG (tel: 0171 837 8838)

Vegetarian Society, Parkdale, Dunham Road, Altringham, Cheshire (tel: 0161 928 0793)

Voluntary Service Overseas (VSO), 317 Putney Bridge Road, London SW15 2PN (tel: 0181 780 2266)

Warner Holidays, 1 Park Lane, Hemel Hempstead, Herts. HP2 4YL (tel: 01442 230300)

Women's Royal Voluntary Service (WRVS), Milton Hill House, Milton Hill, Abingdon, Oxon OX13 6AF

Youth Hostels Association, Trevelyan House, 8 St Stephen's Hill, St Albans, Herts. AL1 2DY (tel: 01793 855215)

Index

The Daily Telegraph

Guide to Lump Sum Investment
11th edition
Liz Walkington

Whether you have won the lottery, received a redundancy payment or inherited a lump sum, you will want to know how to invest the money to make it grow.

This new edition of this comprehensive guide describes the various short- and long-term investment possibilities, whether they are best for capital growth or income, how easy it is to withdraw money, the costs, the most efficient investments for different situations, how safe the money is, likely rates of return and so on. Topics covered in detail include:

- Fixed capital investments
- Gilts
- Equities
- Unit trusts and offshore funds
- Investment trusts
- ISAs
- Life insurance-linked investments
- Pension planning
- Tangible investments
- Charitable giving
- Where to go for advice.

£10.99 • Paperback • ISBN 07494 30125 • 320 pages • 1999

KOGAN PAGE
120 Pentonville Road, London N1 9JN
Tel: 0171 278 0433 • Fax: 0171 837 6348 • www.kogan-page.co.uk

Index of Advertisers

The Daily Telegraph

Guide to Funerals and Bereavement
Sam Weller

Funerals are probably one of the largest yet most unexpected costs that we have to face, yet arranging a funeral usually takes place when the bereaved are at their most vulnerable. Unfortunately, the funeral directing trade is not licensed or regulated and there is concern about the level of pricing and standards. Relatives do not wish to appear mean where their loved ones are concerned so often end up paying more than they can afford.

In this practical book Sam Weller examines the entire 'death care industry'. He provides clear information on arranging a funeral, cremation, burial and memorialization, and the costs involved. He takes a holistic view of death and its aftermath. The book spans:

- **planning for a funeral and what to do when someone dies**
- **memorialization**
- **ownership and inheritance of grave plots**
- **rights and responsibilities in cemeteries and churchyards.**

£8.99 • Paperback • ISBN 0 7494 3057 5 • 208 pages • 1999

KOGAN PAGE
120 Pentonville Road, London N1 9JN
Tel: 0171 278 0433 • Fax: 0171 837 6348 • w w w . k o g a n - p a g e . c o . u k

The Lifeplanner Series

The Lifeplanner series addresses personal finance and consumer issues in a jargon-free, readable way, taking the fear out of planning your life. So whether you are thinking about buying a house, having a baby, getting married or planning your retirement the Lifeplanner series will help you do so wisely.

Titles available are:

Balancing Your Career, Family and Life
Getting Married
Landing Your First Job
Making the Most of Being a Student
The Young Professional's Guide to Personal Finance
Your Child's Education
Your First Home: A Practical Guide to Buying and Renting

Available from all good booksellers. For further information on the series, please contact:

Kogan Page
120 Pentonville Road
London
N1 9JN
Tel: 0171 278 0433
Fax: 0171 837 6348
e-mail: kpinfo@kogan-page.co.uk
or visit our website: www.kogan-page.co.uk

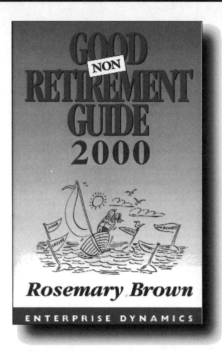

𝕮𝖍𝖊 𝕯𝖆𝖎𝖑𝖞 𝕿𝖊𝖑𝖊𝖌𝖗𝖆𝖕𝖍

Guide to Living Abroad

12th edition
Michael Furnell and Philip Jones

If you have ever dreamed of living abroad, yet worried about the real issues involved, you will find all your questions answered in this new edition of *Living Abroad*. With extensive information on over 20 overseas destinations, this fully revised and updated edition should be your first stop for finding the essential facts about relocating abroad.

You will find practical guidance on:

- **Buying a property abroad**
- **Making arrangements for your UK property**
- **Tax and financial planning**
- **Education**
- **Health matters**
- **Insurance**
- **Language barriers**
- **Returning to the UK.**

£12.99 • Paperback • ISBN 07494 30958 • 392 pages • 1999

KOGAN PAGE
120 Pentonville Road, London N1 9JN
Tel: 0171 278 0433 • Fax: 0171 837 6348 • w w w . k o g a n - p a g e . c o . u k

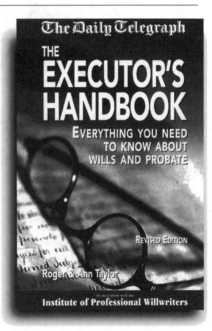